PEDRA BRANCA

The Road to the World Court

PEDRA BRANCA
The Road to the World Court

with best wishes

S Jayakumar and Tommy Koh

with a Foreword by Minister Mentor Lee Kuan Yew

NUS PRESS
SINGAPORE

MFA
DIPLOMATIC
ACADEMY
SINGAPORE

Published by NUS Press in association with the MFA Diplomatic Academy, Ministry of Foreign Affairs

NUS Press
National University of Singapore
AS3-01-02, 3 Arts Link
Singapore 117569

Fax: (65) 6774-0652
E-mail: nusbooks@nus.edu.sg
Website: http://www.nus.edu.sg/npu

ISBN 978-9971-69-457-9 (Paper)
       978-9971-69-474-6 (Case)

National Library Board Singapore Cataloguing in Publication Data

Jayakumar, S.
    Pedra Branca: the road to the world court / S Jayakumar and Tommy Koh. – Singapore: NUS Press in association with the MFA Diplomatic Academy, Ministry of Foreign Affairs, c2009.
    p. cm.
    Includes index.
    ISBN-13: 978-9971-69-474-6
    ISBN-13: 978-9971-69-457-9 (pbk.)

    1. Singapore – Boundaries – Malaysia. 2. Malaysia – Boundaries – Singapore. 3. Territorial waters – Singapore. 4. Territorial waters – Malaysia. 5. Singapore – Foreign relations – Malaysia. 6. Malaysia – Foreign relations – Singapore. I. Koh, Tommy T.B. (Tommy Thong Bee), 1937– II. Title.

KZA1540
341.448095957 — dc22   OCN261364674

Front cover : Pedra Branca (Source: Ministry of Foreign Affairs)

Front flap   : Painting by J.T. Thomson, showing Pedra Branca just after the completion of Horsburgh Lighthouse (1851).

Typeset by : Scientifik Graphics
Printed by : Mainland Press Pte Ltd

CONTENTS

FOREWORD

The Prime Minister must try to establish good, stable and equitable relations with the government of Malaysia. I worked with four successive Malaysian Prime Ministers: Tunku Abdul Rahman, Tun Abdul Razak, Tun Hussein Onn and Tun Dr Mahathir Mohamad.

With our long and close links of family, history, geography and an unfortunate two year experience as part of Malaysia from 1963 to 1965, I knew that relations with Malaysia would have its ups and downs. What is important is how both sides can manage and amicably resolve issues that must crop up from time to time because of our widespread interactions, without souring up our long term overall bilateral relationship. The way the Pedra Branca claim by Malaysia was resolved makes a good case study. It is a story worth telling.

In 1979, Malaysia published a new map on its territorial waters and continental shelf boundaries. In it, Malaysia claimed, for the first time, that Pedra Branca was Malaysian territory. We were surprised because the island had been in British and subsequently Singapore's possession since 1847. There was no protest from Malaysia or any other country for 132 years. We formally protested the 1979 map in February 1980.

But, I saw no need for this claim to trouble our bilateral relationship. I went out of my way to persuade Malaysian PM Hussein Onn, under whose watch this claim was made, to settle this issue in an open and straightforward manner. I found Hussein fair-minded when we discussed the Pedra Branca issue during his visit to Singapore in May 1980. He said both sides should search for documents to prove ownership of Pedra Branca.

Hussein was pre-occupied with domestic matters and the issue was put on a back burner. Dr Mahathir took over in 1981. Mahathir was an activist and drove Malaysia's foreign and domestic policy. We had a good meeting during his first official visit to Singapore in December 1981. This was a turning point in bilateral relations. During that meeting, we agreed that both sides should exchange documents to establish the legitimacy of our respective claims on Pedra Branca. I then left it to Jayakumar, the Attorney-General's Chambers and the Ministry of Foreign Affairs to work with the Malaysians to resolve this issue.

I had seen the key documents and been briefed on the arguments supporting our case. It was clear that we had a very strong legal case. I instructed our then Attorney-General, Tan Boon Teik, to go to Kuala Lumpur and show our documentary evidence to his counterpart, the Malaysian Attorney-General. It was, as Jayakumar and Tommy Koh describe it, an unprecedented unilateral move. I was prepared to take that step to get the Malaysians to know that we had a powerful legal case.

But I also understood that it was difficult for any leader to give up sovereignty claims unilaterally. I therefore proposed to Dr Mahathir in 1989 that if the matter was not settled after an exchange of documents, we should refer the dispute to the International Court of Justice (ICJ).

The two sides then spent many years seeking an amicable solution to the dispute through bilateral discussions. However, these discussions proved futile.

In 1994, Malaysia accepted Singapore's proposal to refer the matter to third-party adjudication, and we settled for the ICJ. This was Singapore's first case in the ICJ. Malaysia had prior experience at the ICJ with the Sipadan and Ligitan case. The judgment of the Court, awarding sovereignty over Pedra Branca to Singapore and sovereignty over Middle Rocks to Malaysia is a partial vindication of Singapore's position. Naturally we were disappointed because we believed, as did our foreign counsel, that any Court would decide that sovereignty over all three features Pedra Branca, Middle Rocks and South Ledge went together.

Nonetheless, the Government accepted the Court's judgment without any qualification. Whichever way the judgment went, it is better for bilateral relations that a conclusive judgment has been made. This allows us to put aside this issue and move on to other areas of cooperation.

Singapore must remain committed to upholding the rule of law in the relations between States. If a dispute cannot be resolved by negotiations, it is better to refer it to a third party dispute settlement mechanism, than to allow it to fester and sour bilateral relations. This was my approach and subsequent Singapore Prime Ministers have continued to subscribe to it.

When Jayakumar and Tommy Koh considered writing up the case, I encouraged them. The Pedra Branca story deserves to be recorded up in a book intelligible to lay readers. Their book recounts the many valuable lessons and insights we have gained from the lengthy negotiations and the final resolution at the ICJ.

Lee Kuan Yew
Minister Mentor, Singapore

PREFACE

For both of us, working on the Pedra Branca case over many years as part of the Singapore team was a labour of love. We had a great interest in public international law. We also felt strongly that Pedra Branca rightfully belonged to Singapore and that Malaysia's belated claim in 1979 had no basis. In the early seventies, we had worked together closely representing Singapore at the Third United Nations Conference on the Law of the Sea (UNCLOS III), which was another labour of love.

UNCLOS III spanned a period of almost ten years (1973–1982) before the new landmark Convention was finally adopted. After UNCLOS III, we collaborated on a writing project and co-authored a comprehensive essay on "The Negotiating Process of the Third United Nations Conference on the Law of the Sea 1982", published by the Center for Oceans Law and Policy, University of Virginia, as part of the Center's project *Third United Nations Convention on the Law of the Sea 1982, A Commentary.*

We conceived the idea of this book on Pedra Branca over a weekend break during the public hearings at The Hague, Netherlands, in November 2007. We had just completed our first round of oral arguments at the International Court of Justice (ICJ) and Malaysia was scheduled to begin its first round of arguments the Tuesday following that weekend.

Over a cup of coffee in our "operations room" at the Crowne Plaza Promenade Hotel, we took stock of the progress of the case. As we reminisced over the many phases of the dispute which, at long last, was drawing to a close, we began to discuss the usefulness of a book where we could record our own impressions of the management of the dispute. Whatever the final decision of the ICJ, this case would certainly be very significant in Singapore's legal history as it was the first time that Singapore had submitted a dispute to the ICJ and we were two of the four Singapore lawyers who had the honour to make presentations to the Court.

Having been members of the team for a long period, we had seen interesting developments as the political, diplomatic and legal phases of the dispute evolved over time. There was an interesting story to tell and we agreed that it would be a good idea for us to collaborate on this writing project just as we had done for our publication on UNCLOS III.

This book is, therefore, the story of the Pedra Branca dispute, of how Britain (and later Singapore as Britain's successor) acquired sovereignty over Pedra Branca and maintained and operated Horsburgh Lighthouse since 1851. It is a story of how the dispute arose after Malaysia made its claim over Pedra Branca in 1979 and how we managed the dispute over a period spanning almost three decades before its final resolution through judgment of the ICJ on 23 May 2008.

We have not attempted a detailed analysis of the legal pleadings and arguments of both countries. Singapore's written pleadings comprised 14 volumes totalling 2,723 pages. Nor have we undertaken an in-depth analysis of the ICJ's final judgment. If we were to attempt to do either, we would be perceived as being biased and partisan. We have decided to leave that task to international law scholars and legal commentators.

We wrote this book to give readers a glimpse of the enormous behind-the-scenes preparations for the case, both before and during the hearings at the ICJ. We hope it will give readers some interesting insights into the way we managed the dispute and the various policy decisions that were made. For example, in the negotiations on the Special Agreement to submit the case to the ICJ, when Malaysia first insisted that Middle Rocks and South Ledge belonged to them, should we agree to their proposal to omit these features from the Agreement? If we had accepted

Malaysia's position, the sovereignty of Middle Rocks and South Ledge would have remained unresolved. Singapore, however, preferred to ask the Court to consider who had sovereignty over the three maritime features. Should we agree to Malaysia's proposal to provide that the ICJ should also decide the rights of the party which was not awarded sovereignty? This would run the risk of the Court deciding to grant sovereignty to Malaysia and to grant only lighthouse operator rights to Singapore.

When Attorney-General Chan Sek Keong was appointed as the Chief Justice, should he continue to represent Singapore as part of the team appearing at The Hague? When one of our international Counsel cautioned that there was a risk that Malaysia would object to our nominating Tommy Koh to be our judge *ad hoc*, should we proceed with our plan and be prepared for the Court to rule against us on preliminary objections even before the actual merits of the case have been heard?

Working on the Pedra Branca case with other colleagues was immensely satisfying and at the same time challenging in many ways. The question put to the ICJ seemed deceptively straight-forward: *"to determine whether sovereignty over (a) Pedra Branca/Pulau Batu Puteh; (b) Middle Rocks; (c) South Ledge; belongs to Malaysia or the Republic of Singapore".* However, as the written pleadings and oral arguments showed, the issues involved in the arguments on who had sovereignty turned not only on legal principles but also on assessing the significance of various historical events in the region as well as the interpretation of treaties, colonial records, maps etc.

What were the factors which contributed to our success in convincing the ICJ to award sovereignty over Pedra Branca to Singapore? There were many and here we will mention the more important factors. Firstly, we were fortunate in assembling a first rate inter-agency team. The absence of turf battles and our ability to subordinate our institutional interests to the national interest is one of Singapore's comparative advantages. It was truly a Singapore Inc or Whole of Government effort. Secondly, from an early stage, we enlisted an excellent team of able international Counsel. Thirdly, close rapport and coordination between the international Counsel and members of the Singapore team proved critical. The international Counsel themselves acknowledged that the quality of their work depended hugely on the input of the Singapore team.

We would add another important factor: we enjoyed the full backing, trust and support from the Prime Minister and his Cabinet. All three Singapore prime ministers, Lee Kuan Yew (1959–1990), Goh Chok Tong (1990–2004) and Lee Hsien Loong (2004–current) followed the case very closely and each of them was *au fait* with the issues. Although they took deep personal interest, they showed full confidence in the team and left it to us and our Counsel to decide the best way to present our case to the ICJ.

The Pedra Branca case was an important development in our bilateral relations with Malaysia. It finally brought closure to this long-standing dispute between the two countries. Beyond bilateral relations, this case served as a good example to the rest of the region on the merits of amicable settlement of disputes through third party adjudication. That approach continues to be an important feature in Singapore's foreign policy in managing disputes with other countries. As Prime Minister Lee Hsien Loong said in his remarks to the media after the ICJ Judgment was made: "This is a good way for us to resolve disagreements or problems while maintaining good relations with each other."

We wish to say a word about the importance of developing international law expertise in Singapore. We are two aging members of the legal fraternity who have dabbled in public international law. We wish to express our conviction that we need to identify early and develop a bigger pool of younger Singaporean lawyers with international law experience and expertise. We need to pay attention to this because of the increasing importance of international law in our foreign relations and the growing demands for international law advice. For example, there is an increasing number of international conferences and forums where our delegations require sound advice on international law. New challenging areas are also emerging, such as climate change. Regardless of whether we have disputes which may find their way to the ICJ or other tribunals, we need to develop a sufficiently large pool of people who are able to respond to such new challenges and operate as credible players in the international arena.

Acknowledgments and Appreciation

We are very grateful to Minister Mentor Lee Kuan Yew for honouring us with his Foreword. We are deeply indebted to Chief Justice Chan Sek Keong who read the manuscript and made many valuable suggestions. We wish to thank our MFA colleagues, Foreign Minister George Yeo, Permanent Secretary Peter Ho, Second Permanent Secretary Bilahari Kausikan, High Commissioner in Kuala Lumpur T Jasudasen and Ambassador in Brussels Anil Kumar Nayar for going through the manuscript and giving many useful comments. Lydia Lim from Singapore Press Holdings, who followed the case closely as a journalist, also gave us good suggestions on earlier drafts.

We are grateful to Sivakant Tiwari, Pang Khang Chau, Foo Chi Hsia, Chang Li Lin, Wu Ye-Min and Stephen Quick for their help and invaluable assistance in the preparation of this book. Stephen and Ye-Min did an outstanding job in checking of facts and tracing documents spanning over 30 years. We also thank Ministry of Information, Communications and the Arts (MICA), Ministry of Defence (MINDEF), Ministry of Foreign Affairs (MFA), Maritime and Port Authority of Singapore (MPA), National Archives of Singapore (NAS) and Tan Ken Hwee for the use of their photographs. We are grateful to the Dean of the MFA Diplomatic Academy, Ho Cheok Sun, for the Academy's support and helping in the book launch. We also appreciate the meticulous editorial work and excellent arrangements of Paul Kratoska from NUS Press.

Finally, we would like to dedicate this book to all the members of the Singapore team, each of whom has made a significant contribution to the success of our collective endeavour.

S Jayakumar and Tommy Koh

CHAPTER 1

HOW IT ALL STARTED

On 23 May 2008, the International Court of Justice (ICJ) gave its judgment on the case "*Sovereignty over Pedra Branca/Pulau Batu Puteh, Middle Rocks and South Ledge*", which Singapore and Malaysia had by Special Agreement referred to the ICJ on 24 July 2003. The ICJ decided that sovereignty over Pedra Branca belonged to Singapore.[1] That decision effectively put an end to a dispute between both countries which had spanned some three decades. During this period, both sides had to manage the issue so that it would not seriously damage overall bilateral relations.

How did it all start? The dispute over Pedra Branca[2] between Singapore and Malaysia was formally triggered off on 21 December 1979, when Malaysia published its now infamous

---

[1] The ICJ found that sovereignty over Pedra Branca/Pulau Batu Puteh belongs to the Republic of Singapore and that sovereignty over Middle Rocks belongs to Malaysia. The Court also found that South Ledge belongs to the State in the territorial waters of which it is located.

[2] As Tommy Koh told the ICJ in his opening speech on 6 November 2007 as Agent, "'Pedra Branca' means 'white rock' in the Portuguese language. The phrase 'Pulau Batu Puteh' means 'white rock island' in the Malay language. The whitish appearance is caused by the accumulation of bird droppings over hundreds of years. The name Pulau Batu Puteh has only recently appeared in maps of the region and is the name by which my Malaysian friends refer to the island today."

Pedra Branca
(Source: Ministry of Foreign Affairs, Singapore)

map which for the first time included Pedra Branca as part of Malaysian territory. Shortly after the publication of this map, the Singapore Government issued a formal protest to Malaysia on 14 February 1980.

However, our suspicion that Malaysia was likely to make such a claim had been aroused before they published the 1979 map. In March 1977, Lieutenant Commander Mak Siew Wah from the Hydrographic Branch, Royal Malaysian Navy, made an inquiry to Singapore's Hydrographer, N N Sathaye, regarding the status of Pedra Branca.

The Indonesian Justice Minister, Mochtar Kusumaatmadja, raised a similar query in October 1977, asking whether Malaysia intended to claim Pedra Branca, which might result in a dispute with Singapore. This telling comment was made during a meeting of officials in Jakarta to discuss bilateral matters including the Indonesian archipelagic concept. Mochtar mentioned that if

Pedra Branca belonged to Singapore, she (Singapore) would be entitled to an Exclusive Economic Zone (EEZ) around Pedra Branca almost the size of Singapore.

In April 1978, Kishore Mahbubani (who was then Counsellor at our High Commission in Kuala Lumpur) sent a report to the Ministry of Foreign Affairs (MFA) where he concluded that Malaysia wanted to claim sovereignty over the island on which Horsburgh Lighthouse had stood since 1851. Reporting a conversation with Malaysia's Principal Assistant Secretary in charge of Southeast Asia, Halim Ali, Kishore said that the Malaysians claimed to have completed a study showing that Horsburgh Lighthouse belonged to Malaysia. Halim Ali cited two arguments: first, under the treaty by which the Sultan of Johor ceded Singapore to the East India Company, Singapore was allowed to claim a territorial sea of three nautical miles and Horsburgh Lighthouse lay outside this three miles limit. Second, he said there was a letter which showed that the British were granted permission only to build and maintain a lighthouse on the island. The letter did not state that the British would be granted sovereignty over the island. In his report,[3] Kishore said that Malaysia would be writing to Singapore officially to claim sovereignty over the island. However, we did not receive any written communication.

These developments led our Foreign Ministry to conclude that something was clearly afoot. The Government wisely decided to look into the legal position and ensure that we had all the historical documents relevant to establish the legal basis of our ownership of Pedra Branca.

At that time, Jayakumar was still teaching in the Faculty of Law of the University of Singapore. He had returned to the Faculty in 1974 after completing his term as Permanent Representative to the United Nations (UN). His colleague in the Faculty, Tommy Koh, succeeded him at the UN (it was his

---

[3] Kishore's note is quoted in Singapore's pleadings — *Reply of Singapore*, Case concerning Sovereignty over Pedra Branca/Pulau Batu Puteh, Middle Rocks and South Ledge (Malaysia/Singapore), Volume 3, Annex 51.

second term as Permanent Representative to the UN). Jayakumar continued to assist the Foreign Ministry as a member of the delegation to the Third United Nations Conference on the Law of the Sea (UNCLOS III). Other members of the team were Tommy Koh, Sivakant Tiwari and Chao Hick Tin (now Judge of Appeal of the Supreme Court of Singapore), all of whom later formed part of our Pedra Branca team. The venue for these meetings alternated between the offices of the UN in New York and Geneva.

In May 1978, when the team was in Geneva for the 7th Session of UNCLOS III, Jayakumar received an urgent note from MFA's Deputy Secretary, Tan Boon Seng, informing him of these developments. MFA requested him to head for London to search for certain documents that they had not been able to locate in Singapore.

They were particularly interested in locating the original of the 1844 letter written by the Governor of the Straits Settlements Colonel W J Butterworth to Raja Ali (Sultan Hussein's heir) and the Temenggong of Johor, which the Malaysians were probably relying on as evidence that the British sought permission from the Malay rulers only to build a lighthouse on Pedra Branca. After consulting Tommy, Jayakumar took time off from the meetings in Geneva and spent a few days researching at both the India House (India Office Library and Records, London) as well as the Public Record Office (Kew). That was the beginning of Jayakumar's 30-year involvement in the Pedra Branca saga.

Jayakumar made two separate trips to London to search for various records but he was unable to locate the 1844 letter written by Governor Butterworth. He did locate copies of the replies from Raja Ali and the Temenggong, and he also retrieved several other documents dated 1844 that referred to Peak Rock (another island) but not Pedra Branca.

He sent all these documents and his comments back to Singapore. From his examination of this material it became clear that the British had first considered building a lighthouse on Peak Rock. We therefore concluded that the correspondence between Butterworth and the Johor rulers was in fact about Peak Rock. The British did not seek Johor's permission to build Horsburgh Lighthouse on Pedra Branca because, as we argued before the Court, they did not consider that the island belonged to the Malay rulers. Moreover, Pedra Branca fell outside the three miles territorial sea limit of Johor. As we will show later, this was a very important point in the case.

As an aside, Jayakumar was very impressed with the careful and systematic way the British had preserved their vast array of colonial records. He was also amazed at the meticulous manner that officials of the British Government and East India Company of the 18th and 19th centuries dutifully kept records of all their correspondences between the authorities in the Straits Settlements (including Singapore), in London and also in Bengal, India. In those days, there were no typewriters, fax machines or photocopiers. Copies of every letter and official minutes were transcribed by hand in neat manuscript form. This was no mean feat considering the many colonial possessions Britain had at the height of the Empire.

Another interesting observation, recorded in Jayakumar's report to MFA at that time, was that at both the India Office and at the Public Record Office in Kew, the staff asked if he was the person who had come two days before requesting similar documents. Jayakumar concluded from this that the Malaysians were searching for the same materials.

CHAPTER 2

THE ISSUES

"Pedra Branca, lying in the middle of the eastern entrance of Singapore strait, nearly 8 miles from either shore, is 24 feet (7^{m}3) high. It is on the western edge of a bank with depths of 6 to 10 fathoms (11^{m}0 to 18^{m}3), which extends 1$^1/_4$ miles eastward of it. It will be known by the lighthouse, which was erected on it in 1851, and named after Horsburgh, the celebrated hydrographer, whose labours have in a high degree benefited the interests of navigation and commerce in every part of the eastern seas."

Source: Malacca Strait Pilot, 1924[4]

The Physical and Geographical Setting

The reader may find it useful to understand the physical and geographical context of the dispute. Pedra Branca is an island measuring 137 metres long, with an average width of 60 metres and covers an area of about 8,560 square metres at low tide. There is no evidence that Pedra Branca was ever inhabited before the British constructed Horsburgh Lighthouse on it. After the construction, personnel manning the lighthouse lived on the island.

---

[4] The *Malacca Strait Pilot* is an information book that describes coasts, waters, channels, harbour facilities.

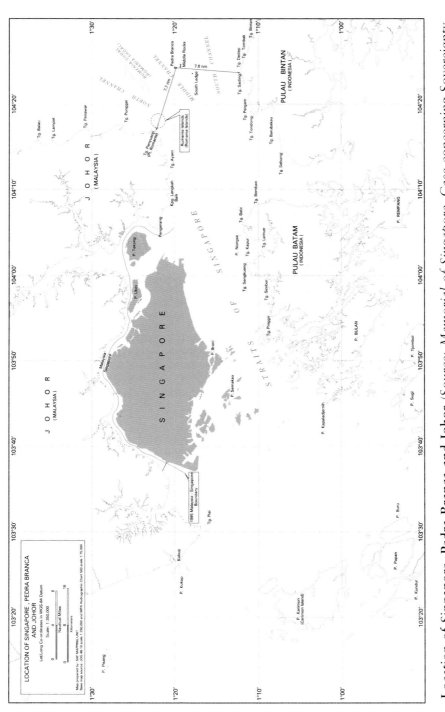

Location of Singapore, Pedra Branca and Johor (Source: *Memorial of Singapore, Case concerning Sovereignty over Pedra Branca/Pulau Batu Puteh, Middle Rocks and South Ledge* (Malaysia/Singapore), Volume 1, Map 2).

Vessels passing through the waters around Pedra Branca
(Source: Ministry of Foreign Affairs, Singapore)

Pedra Branca lies 24 nautical miles to the east of Singapore (1°19.8'N, 104°24.4'E), at the eastern entrance to the Straits of Singapore. It sits almost exactly in the middle of the Straits (7.7 nautical miles from the Southern coast of Johor (Malaysia) to the north and 7.6 nautical miles from the northern coast of Bintan (Indonesia) to the south).

Due to its location in the middle of the Straits of Singapore as it opens into the South China Sea, Pedra Branca has always posed a serious navigational hazard on an important international trade route. Between 1824 and 1851, 16 ships were wrecked and another nine stranded after running aground in the vicinity of Pedra Branca. As such, the island had long been of strategic significance to shipping from India to China and vice-versa, a point made by J T Thomson, the Government Surveyor who designed and constructed the lighthouse on Pedra Branca, in his account of the Horsburgh Lighthouse. The lighthouse on the island has served the international shipping community well by warning it of this hazard in one of the busiest shipping lanes of the world.

**Painting by J T Thomson, showing Pedra Branca just after the
completion of Horsburgh Lighthouse (1851)**
(Source: *Memorial of Singapore*, Case concerning Sovereignty over
Pedra Branca/Pulau Batu Puteh, Middle Rocks and South Ledge
(Malaysia/Singapore), Volume 1, Image 2).

Today, more than 150 years later, this significance has
not diminished. The Straits of Singapore is one of the busiest
international straits in the world. It links the Straits of Malacca
(and the Indian Ocean to the West) with the South China Sea
(and the Pacific Ocean to the East). As a result, most ships going
to the Far East from Europe, the Middle East and India, and
vice versa, pass through the Straits of Singapore. On average,
more than 900 ships use the Straits of Singapore each day (one
ship every 1.6 minutes) with more than 80 per cent of these
ships arriving and departing from the port of Singapore, making
Singapore the busiest port in the world. At any one time, more
than 1,000 ships are within the limits of the port of Singapore.
As Pedra Branca commands the entire eastern approach to the
Straits, the continued ability of Singapore to exercise her sovereign
territorial rights over Pedra Branca and its surrounding waters
is of utmost importance to Singapore.

British Acquisition of Pedra Branca and Building of the Lighthouse

Singapore's case was that the acquisition of Pedra Branca took place some 160 years ago when the British colonial government in Singapore decided to build a lighthouse on Pedra Branca. The British Government took possession of the island in 1847 and proceeded to build a lighthouse named in memory of the eminent Hydrographer, James Horsburgh FRS. Actual construction of the lighthouse began in 1850 and the lighthouse commenced operations the following year. We argued that, by the time the lighthouse was completed, Britain had acquired sovereignty over Pedra Branca. Horsburgh Lighthouse was in fact the first lighthouse to be built by the British in Southeast Asia.

Pedra Branca was described as a dependency of Singapore at the lighthouse foundation stone ceremony held in May 1850 in the presence of the British Governor. British ownership of the island was also recognised by the Dutch, the other colonial power in the region at the time. The Dutch had, in their internal official correspondence in November that year described it as "British territory". The lighthouse was inaugurated in October 1851. Two months later, in 1852, the Government of India passed a law that vested the lighthouse and its appurtenances in the East India Company, an arrangement later replaced by legislation that reiterated the vesting of the property in the East India Company. Both laws could only be passed if the Government of India considered Pedra Branca as British territory.

We maintained that, after acquiring sovereignty over Pedra Branca, the British and later the Singapore Government (as successor to Britain) undertook a full range of acts of sovereignty and jurisdiction on the island and in its waters. These included: notices to Mariners; the constant maintenance and expansion of the facilities on the island including construction of jetties, a helicopter landing pad, radar and communications facilities; reclamation plans; the collection of meteorological data; the flying of the ensign; numerous visits by high-ranking Singapore

Singapore's marine ensign at Pedra Branca (Source: Tan Ken Hwee)

officials; control of access by Singapore of foreigners, including Malaysian nationals, to the island; the issuance of permits to third parties to undertake scientific research and salvage operations; the exercise of jurisdiction to investigate shipping incidents and accidental deaths; and more.

Singapore continuously acted as a country that had sovereignty over the island. In contrast, Malaysia had performed no sovereign acts, had repeatedly recognised Singapore's title over Pedra Branca, and had attributed Pedra Branca to Singapore in several maps and meteorological studies.

Johor's Express Disclaimer of Title to Pedra Branca

An important point was an express disclaimer of title to Pedra Branca. This extremely important statement was given in 1953 when the Acting State Secretary of Johor declared, in a letter of 21 September to the Colonial Secretary of Singapore, that "the Johor Government does not claim ownership of Pedra Branca".

The 1953 correspondence was sent in response to an enquiry made on 12 June 1953 on behalf of the Colonial Secretary, Singapore, by J D Higham, Under-Secretary in the Colonial Secretary's Office. Higham's letter was addressed to the British Adviser and copied to the Chief Secretary of the Federation of Malaya. This letter explained that the Colonial Secretary of Singapore, was seeking "… information about the rock some 40 miles from Singapore known as Pedra Branca on which the Horsburgh Lighthouse stands," this being "… relevant to the determination of the boundaries of the Colony's territorial waters". Higham went on to state that this rock was outside the limits ceded to the East India Company with the island of Singapore in the 1824 Treaty and was mentioned in a despatch from the Governor of Singapore of 28 November 1844 (an extract from which was enclosed as Annex B to Higham's letter of 12 June 1953).

Higham continued by referring to the lighthouse "built in 1850 by the Colony Government who have maintained it ever since". He commented that this, by international usage, no doubt "confers some rights and obligations on the Colony [of Singapore]". Higham concluded by stressing the desirability of clarifying the status of Pedra Branca and by enquiring:

> "… whether there is any document showing a lease or grant of the rock or whether it has been ceded by the Government of the State of Johor or in any other way disposed of."

An immediate response to Higham's letter of 12 June 1953 came in an incompletely dated letter of June 1953 from J D Turner, Secretary to the Johor British Adviser. Turner's letter explained to the Colonial Secretary, Singapore, that the British Adviser in Johor had passed on his letter of 12 June to the State Secretary "… to whom it should, in the British Adviser's opinion, have been addressed in so far as Johor [was] concerned".

This exchange culminated in a reply letter of 21 September 1953 from M Seth bin Saaid, Acting State Secretary of Johor

MC

CSO.11692/52/

CSO.11692/52/   12ᵗʰ June,   1953

The Honourable
The British Adviser,
JOHORE.

Sir,

        I am directed to ask for information about the
rock some 40 miles from Singapore known as Pedra Branca
on which the Horsburgh Lighthouse stands. The matter is
relevant to the determination of the boundaries of the
Colony's territorial waters. It appears this rock is
outside the limits ceded by Sultan Hussain and the Dato
Tumunggong to the East India Company with the island of
Singapore in the Treaty of 1824 (extract at 'A'). It
was however mentioned in a despatch from the Governor of
Singapore on 28th November 1844 (extract at 'B'). The
lighthouse was built in 1850 by the Colony Government
who have maintained it ever since. This by international
usage no doubt confers some rights and obligations on the
Colony.

2.   In the case of Pulau Pisang which is also outside the Treaty limits of the Colony it has been possible
to trace an indenture in the Johore Registry of Deeds
dated 6th October, 1900. This shows that a part of Pulau
Pisang was granted to the Crown for the purposes of
building a lighthouse. Certain conditions were attached
and it is clear that there was no abrogation of the
sovereignty of Johore. The status of Pisang is quite
clear.

3.   It is now desired to clarify the status of Pedra
Branca. I would therefore be most grateful to know whether
there is any document showing a lease or grant of the rock
or whether it has been ceded by the Government of the State
of Johore or in any other way disposed of.

4.   A copy of this letter is being sent to the Chief
Secretary, Kuala Lumpur.

                I am, Sir,
                  Your obedient servant,

                    JOHN D HIGHAM

                   (J.D. Higham)
              for Colonial Secretary,
                  Singapore.

c.c.to:-

The Honourable
The Chief Secretary,
Federation of Malaya,
KUALA LUMPUR.

Letter from J D Higham, on behalf of the Singapore Colonial Secretary
to the British Adviser, Johor, dated 12 June 1953 (Source: *Memorial of
Singapore*, Case concerning Sovereignty over Pedra Branca/Pulau Batu Puteh,
Middle Rocks and South Ledge (Malaysia/Singapore), Volume 6, Annex 93).

It is requested that the
following number be quoted
in reply to this letter.

No. SSJ.1120/53/6

Tel. S.B. 92616 or 92801 Ex. 36
U.S. 92656 or 92801 Ex. 24
A.S. 92801 Ex. 25

STATE SECRETARY'S OFFICE,
JOHORE,

JOHORE BAHRU, ...21st Sept....... 19 53.

Sir,   COLONIAL SECRETARIAT
                    RECEIVED

            I have the honour to refer to your letter
No.CSO.11692/52 dated 12th June 1953, addressed
to the British Adviser, Johore, on the question
of the status of Pedra Branca Rock some 40 miles
from Singapore and to inform you that the Johore
Government does not claim ownership of Pedra
Branca.

                    I have the honour to be,
                              Sir,
                    Your obedient servant,

                    (M. SETH BIN SAAID)
                    AG: STATE SECRETARY
                              JOHORE.

To:
    The Hon'ble
    The Colonial Secretary,
    Singapore.

TA:B.

Letter from M Seth Bin Saaid (Acting State Secretary of Johor) to
the Colonial Secretary, Singapore, dated 21 September 1953
(Source: *Memorial of Singapore*, Case concerning Sovereignty over
Pedra Branca/Pulau Batu Puteh, Middle Rocks and South Ledge
(Malaysia/Singapore), Volume 6, Annex 96).

to the Colonial Secretary, Singapore. This letter informed the Colonial Secretary, Singapore that:

"... *the Johore Government does not claim ownership of Pedra Branca.*"

This 1953 letter formed an important part of Singapore's case. We argued that it showed that Johor officials never regarded Pedra Branca as belonging to Johor. It was also a declaration that Johor or its successor state, Malaysia, in future would not assert any claim on Pedra Branca. As we stated in our pleadings, this letter put to rest the status of Pedra Branca *vis-à-vis* Johor, and therefore Malaysia. The validity of this letter has never been questioned. The letter itself has also never been retracted at any time. The answer of the Acting State Secretary formed the basis of an express mutual understanding between Singapore and Johor on the status of Pedra Branca, a mutual understanding that went unquestioned until Malaysia sought to deny it 26 years later by publishing the 1979 Territorial Waters and Continental Shelf Boundaries Map. It was only at the end of the oral hearings that Malaysia tried to argue that the Acting State Secretary was neither authorised nor had the legal capacity to write the 1953 letter. This belated argument was that its content concerned foreign affairs, which was under the charge of the Federal Government under the 1948 Federation of Malaya Agreement.[5]

Malaysian Maps

Another significant fact was that Malaysia had published a number of maps which were in our favour. In 1962, the Federation of Malaya published two official maps that attributed Pedra Branca to Singapore. In 1965 (the year Singapore left the Federation

---

[5] See also Chapter 11 "Malaysian Attorney-General's New Argument" and Singapore's reply to the Question posed by Judge Keith at Annex B.

of Malaysia), and again in 1974 and 1975, Malaysia published official maps attributing Pedra Branca to Singapore by depicting Pedra Branca with the notes "Singapore" or "Singapura".

Emergence of Malaysia's Claim

In 1978, two Malaysian surveyors attempted to land on Pedra Branca. They left the island when directed by the lighthouse keeper to do so. The Malaysian Ministry of Foreign Affairs took this matter up in passing with the Singapore High Commission in Malaysia at a meeting in April 1978. This is the meeting mentioned in Chapter 1. At that meeting, the Malaysian official also claimed to have made a study showing that Pedra Branca belonged to Malaysia. The Singapore official, Kishore Mahbubani, responded unequivocally that Pedra Branca belonged to Singapore.

Therefore, it was only in 1978 that we began to see Malaysia taking the first tentative steps towards asserting a claim to Pedra Branca. It was also only in 1979 that Malaysia made a formal claim to the island through the publication of its map entitled "Territorial Waters and Continental Shelf Boundaries of Malaysia".

On the day the map was published, Singapore's High Commissioner to Malaysia, Wee Kim Wee, was summoned to meet with a senior official of the Malaysian Ministry of Foreign Affairs. At that meeting, the Malaysian official read out a typewritten official statement concerning the publication of the 1979 map. He did not provide a copy of the statement to Singapore High Commissioner Wee. He did not even provide the High Commissioner with a copy of the 1979 map! Instead, the High Commissioner was asked to buy his own copy of the map from the Map Sales Office. Nor did the Malaysian official come straight to the point about Pedra Branca. It was only after he had put aside his typewritten statement and answered a few questions from Wee that he admitted that, in the case of Singapore, Pedra Branca was affected by the map.

Map entitled "Territorial Waters and Continental Shelf Boundaries of Malaysia", published by the Director of National Mapping, Malaysia (1979) (Composite of Sheets 1 and 2)

(Source: *Memorial of Singapore*, Case concerning Sovereignty over Pedra Branca/Pulau Batu Puteh, Middle Rocks and South Ledge (Malaysia/Singapore), Volume 1, Map 7).

Singapore was, of course, quite surprised by Malaysia's belated attempt to claim Pedra Branca, given Singapore's long-standing and unopposed title and sovereignty over the island.

MFA immediately assembled its inter-ministry team of experts to study the latest Malaysian map and its implications for Singapore. As it turned out, in addition to the claim over Pedra Branca, in this map, Malaysia had also made unacceptable territorial sea claims against Singapore at the eastern and western ends of the main island. These claims were marked as Point 20[6] and Point 23 in the extract of the 1979 map. These two claims created sharp and unusual slivers cutting deeply into Singapore's territorial sea at the eastern and western ends.

In fact, Malaysia's 1979 map affected not just Singapore. The map attracted protests from as many as seven neighbouring countries — Brunei, China, Indonesia, the Philippines, Singapore, Thailand and Vietnam. In February 1980, Singapore issued a diplomatic note that not only protested against Malaysia's claim to Pedra Branca but also protested Malaysia's claim in relation to Point 20 and Point 23. In that note, Singapore said:

> "The Government of the Republic of Singapore is gravely concerned at what is set out in the said map. This map purports to claim the island of Pedra Branca as belonging to Malaysia. The Government of the Republic of Singapore rejects this claim. There is no premise in international law on which to found such a claim. The Government of the Republic of Singapore has since the 1840s, by virtue of both its acts and those of its predecessor governments, occupied and exercised sovereignty over Pedra Branca and the waters around it. Since that time, no other country has exercised or claimed jurisdiction or contested Singapore's sovereignty over Pedra Branca. The Government of the Republic of Singapore

---

[6] The dispute concerning Point 20 was raised in the reclamation case which Malaysia brought against Singapore in the International Tribunal for the Law of the Sea (ITLOS).

therefore requests that the said map be suitably amended to
reflect the sovereignty of Singapore over Pedra Branca."

With this formal protest by Singapore, it can be said that the
dispute over Pedra Branca had crystallised.[7]

---

[7] In its judgment on 23 May 2008, the Court ruled that the "critical date"
as regards the dispute on Pedra Branca was 14 February 1980, the time
when Singapore protested the 1979 Malaysian map. As regards the critical
date for the Middle Rocks and South Ledge dispute, the Court ruled that
it was 6 February 1993 when Singapore referred to these issues in bilateral
discussions.

CHAPTER 3

THE POLITICAL AND DIPLOMATIC PHASE

The decision by both countries to refer the dispute to the ICJ was not taken until some 14 years after the dispute arose in 1980.

During these 14 years, the Pedra Branca issue continued to be an irritant in bilateral relations. Our approach in those early years was to persuade Malaysia that we had a strong legal case with sound arguments on our side. It was our hope that they would recognise that they had a weak case and that it was really futile for them to press their claim. This was the reason we had proposed that both sides exchange documents so that each side could appreciate the strengths and weaknesses of the other's case.

We went so far as to let them have sight of our documents unilaterally before seeing theirs. This was arranged through the two Attorneys General in 1989. We did this because we wanted to resolve this with Malaysia without acrimony or tensions. Our Attorney-General, Tan Boon Teik, had a very good working relationship with his counterpart the Attorney-General of Malaysia, Tan Sri Datuk Abu Talib bin Othman. In July 1989, Abu Talib informally requested to have sight of the documents we had that supported our case on sovereignty over Pedra Branca.

Tan Boon Teik, after consulting Government, arranged to meet Abu Talib (from 24–25 July 1989) in Kuala Lumpur to hand him our documents as part of a "Memorandum on Singapore's case over Pedra Branca" (which included the 1953 disclaimer by Johor). At the request of Wisma Putra, this meeting was kept informal. While Tan Boon Teik handed the documents to Abu Talib on the understanding that Abu Talib could show them only to the Prime Minister, Dr Mahathir Mohamad, it became evident later that the documents were sent to Wisma Putra.[8] After the meeting, Tan Boon Teik reported that, after examining the documents, Abu Talib expressed the view that Malaysia had a weak case.

Defusing Tensions Created by Dangerous Incidents

Meanwhile, in the mid and late eighties, the need to find a political solution to the dispute became even more urgent when Royal Malaysian Marine Police boats began to make regular intrusions into Pedra Branca waters. These appeared to be deliberate attempts made belatedly by Malaysia either to assert or to build up a claim to sovereignty over Pedra Branca and its surrounding waters.

We became concerned when actions of the Malaysian vessels became increasingly provocative and potentially dangerous. From June to July 1989, the Malaysian vessels came ever closer to Pedra Branca, sometimes coming into its waters at high speeds. Instead of just sailing around the island, the ships anchored in our waters and also took photographs of Horsburgh Lighthouse. Our officials observed that the personnel on these vessels were

---

[8] This is clear from the conversation between Wisma Putra's Secretary-General, Tan Sri Ahmad Kamil Jaafar and Permanent Secretary for Foreign Affairs, Peter Chan on 22 August 1990. Peter Chan reported that during this conversation, Kamil Jaafar said that "after receiving the documents from you", a research team had been sent to India and the UK and had also visited Johor to look at all the evidence.

**Republic of Singapore Navy vessel patrolling waters off
Pedra Branca** (Source: Ministry of Defence, Singapore)

armed with pistols and M-16 rifles. In fact, one of the vessels that
anchored one nautical mile from Pedra Branca had its General
Purpose Machine Gun loaded with a belt of ammunition. This
was a departure from normal practice.

Such incidents created tense situations on the ground. Our
Navy was under strict instructions to avoid escalating matters.
We were concerned not to let the situation get out of hand.
With armed Malaysian boats coming into close quarters and
seemingly encountering our naval vessels, there was always a
danger of an accident or miscalculation — something which
both countries clearly ought to avoid.

The following transcript[9] of a radio communication of a
typical incident between a Singapore Navy vessel and a Malaysian

---

[9] Transcript of radio conversation between Singapore Navy vessel RSS Daring
and Malaysian Police vessel PZ 5.

Police vessel (at 0040 hrs on 16 June 1989) illustrates the nature of the incidents which took place. It shows that the intrusion was deliberate and under instructions. The restraint exercised by our Navy is evident from the transcript:

RSS vessel	*Hello Selamat Malam. Can I speak to your CO?*
Malaysian Vessel	*Good evening.*
RSS vessel	*I am directed by my authorities to remind you that you are in Singapore territorial waters. Your activities here are inconsistent with innocent passage or transit passage. Please leave this area. Have you received my message?*
Malaysian Vessel	*I receive your message loud and clear. As I've told your previous patrol boat commander, we were directed by our authorities to be here. According to the Malaysian Government, this is clear Malaysian territorial waters … so far as the Malaysian Government is concerned, this was developed [sic] in Malaysia and I have been specifically directed to be in this area – over.*
RSS vessel	*… Your message is received. I will convey your message to the authorities. Thank you for your attention.*
Malaysian Vessel	*Thank you.*

To prevent an escalation of such tensions or, worse, an ugly confrontation, we made approaches to Malaysia at various levels. Officially, our High Commission in Kuala Lumpur issued three diplomatic notes to Malaysia's Ministry of Foreign Affairs to protest the intrusions while expressing our willingness to seek an amicable resolution.

Messages were also conveyed through well placed diplomatic and political channels to the Malaysian Prime Minister that the situation was too risky if the Malaysian Marine Police continued with their actions. For example, our High Commissioner in Kuala Lumpur, S R Nathan, was instructed to express our concerns to the Malaysian Finance Minister Datuk Paduka Daim Zainuddin, who was known to be close to Malaysian Prime Minister Dr Mahathir.

In addition, Foreign Minister Wong Kan Seng also met his Malaysian counterpart, Dato Haji Abu Hassan Bin Haji Omar, twice on 16 June 1989 and 17 July 1989. During the meeting on 16 June 1989, Wong Kan Seng handed over two Third Party Notes (TPNs).[10] These diplomatic notes reiterated Singapore's sovereignty over Pedra Branca and the waters surrounding it. The notes further protested against the provocative activities by Malaysian Police boats, which clearly did not amount to innocent or transit passage. Wong Kan Seng also expressed concerns on these and other matters, including arrests of Singapore vessels. The 17 July 1989 meeting took place just one week before the meeting of the two Attorneys General. Wong Kan Seng informed Abu Hassan that Attorney-General Tan Boon Teik had accepted Attorney-General Abu Talib's invitation. At that meeting, Wong Kan Seng also told his Malaysian counterpart that Tan Boon Teik had full authority to discuss Pedra Branca with Abu Talib and show him our documents.

The Malaysians eventually withdrew their Royal Malaysian Marine Police boats from Pedra Branca, but that did not reduce the imperative for us to seek a solution to the dispute at the political level or even at a legal level, including through third-party adjudication. While the immediate stand-off was

---

[10] Foreign Minister Wong handed over two TPNs during the meeting on 16 June 1989. TPN SHC 98/99 was our protest in relation to the arrest of eight Singapore-registered fishing vessels by Malaysia. TPN SHC 99/89 was our protest over the intrusion of a Malaysian Police Boat and its seaboat into Pedra Branca waters on 14 June 1989.

over, intrusions into the waters of Pedra Branca by Malaysian vessels continued to be a matter of concern over the years. (See Chapter 5.)

Pedra Branca also Became a Political Issue in Malaysia

It was not only intrusions by Malaysian vessels that gave rise to concern. Every now and then, Pedra Branca would emerge as a local issue in Malaysian politics, with various parties urging their Government to staunchly defend Malaysia's interests. As it was part of their internal politics, we were careful not to over-react. However, where necessary, MFA did issue press releases to rebut statements made by the United Malays National Organisation (UMNO) asserting Malaysia's sovereignty.[11]

Sometimes, when such political statements threatened to be accompanied by actions on the ground, it was a cause for serious concern.

On 21 May 1992, the media reported that Parti Islam SeMalaysia (PAS) Youth, probably wanting to upstage UMNO Youth, had planned to plant a Malaysian flag on Pedra Branca. The next day, Malaysian media carried MFA's firm warning to PAS that any intruders would be arrested and charged with illegal entry.

Fortunately, Malaysian authorities also saw the dangers of such actions. Malaysian police thwarted PAS Youth's attempts by telling a group of 35 PAS members at Pengerang to cancel their plans.

---

[11] Our press statement, released on 16 September 1991, welcomed the statement of the Malaysian Deputy Minister of Foreign Affairs, Dato Dr Abdullah Fadzil Che Wan, that Malaysia was ready for talks with Singapore on the Pedra Branca issue and that a third party should be asked to help resolve the matter if Malaysia and Singapore could not resolve it themselves. We also welcomed the statements by the Malaysian Deputy Minister of Foreign Affairs and the Menteri Besar of Johor, Tan Sri Muhyiddin Yassin, that their government was ready to provide evidence of Malaysia's claim to Pedra Branca.

Dr Mahathir also ticked off PAS Youth and in so doing gave a clear signal to the Malaysians that matters should not be allowed to get out of hand. He warned that actions such as planting the Malaysian flag on Pedra Branca could start a war.

> *"The Prime Minister emphasised that attempts by members of the [PAS] to plant a flag on the island recently may not only damage Malaysia-Singapore relations but could also drag the country to war. He said the action was provocative and ought not to be done by the party.*
>
> *"Their actions appear to be inviting people to war. What if others from other countries attempt to plant their flags on islands belonging to us," he said in a news conference after chairing the UMNO Supreme Council meeting here today."*
>
> *Source: Utusan Malaysia, 9 June 1992*

Clearly, Dr Mahathir was aware of the need not to let the situation get out of control. In 1989, he himself had taken an unannounced boat trip to the vicinity of Pedra Branca to personally size up the situation. Dr Mahathir disclosed this fact in an address to the Banker's Club in Kuala Lumpur on 10 June 2008. He said that his boat was immediately intercepted by two Singapore naval vessels. Since he did not want to cause an international incident, he asked his own boat to leave.[12]

Discussions between Prime Ministers

Due to the political sensitivity and gravity of the Pedra Branca issue, it featured in several discussions at the highest levels between the Prime Ministers of both countries when they met for bilateral discussions or on the sidelines at international Conferences.

---

[12] Based on the report from an official of the Singapore High Commission who was present at the function. Diplomats were present as guests and members of The Banker's Club.

Malaysian PM Hussein Onn and Singapore PM Lee Kuan Yew
hold press conference at the Istana during Malaysian PM's visit
to Singapore (13 May 1980) (Source: Ministry of Information,
Communications and the Arts, Singapore; Courtesy of
National Archives of Singapore)

Meeting between PM Lee Kuan Yew and PM Hussein Onn (13 May 1980)

The Prime Ministers of Malaysia and Singapore met in May
1980, and among the topics discussed was Pedra Branca.
Malaysia's Prime Minister, Hussein Onn, explained the reason
for Malaysia's unilateral action in publishing the map. He said
it did not mean that they would take possession of islands or
areas which were included in the map when other countries said
they equally had claim to them. He promised that both sides
would go back to see whether there were documents to prove
to which country the island really belonged.

An interesting disclosure was made at the press conference
which the two leaders held on 13 May 1980 at the Istana. When
asked about Malaysia's claim to Pedra Branca, Prime Minister
Hussein Onn gave an ambivalent response:

"As regards Singapore, I think this is especially in connection with the Batu Puteh ... (pause) ... Pulau Batu Puteh ... Branca ... (pause) ... Pedra Branca, on which there is the lighthouse by the name of Horsburgh, and I have mentioned this to Mr Lee Kuan Yew, saying that we have received your note with regard to the island and let's talk. And this is the question of producing ... I think Mr Lee Kuan Yew is aware ... this is a question of going back into whatever documents there are, to prove who, to which nation, to which country this island really belong in the light of whatever documents may be available.

And I think Mr Lee Kuan Yew says ... (pause) ... he has got ... (pause) ... some documents. We are also looking into the question because this is not very clear to us with regard to this island and we include that in the ... (sudden pause) .... If there are any evidences to that effect, we are willing and prepared to settle this thing peacefully, amicably."

At the ICJ's oral hearings, we played the sound recording of the full extract of Prime Minister Hussein Onn's comments on Pedra Branca. Both Chao Hick Tin[13] and Jayakumar[14] told the Court that such an ambivalent answer from the Prime Minister was not consistent with Malaysia's assertion of sovereignty over Pedra Branca, especially coming so soon after Malaysia's publication of the 1979 map and Singapore's protest.

Meeting between PM Lee Kuan Yew and PM Dr Mahathir Mohamad (17 December 1981)

The matter was discussed between the Singapore Prime Minister, Lee Kuan Yew, and Dr Mahathir in December 1981 during the

---

[13] CR 2007/20, 6 November 2007, pp. 34–35, para. 43–44 (Chao). [Note: For all Court Record (CR) references, please refer to Verbatim Records, Oral Pleadings of Singapore, Case concerning Sovereignty over Pedra Branca/Pulau Batu Puteh, Middle Rocks and South Ledge (Malaysia/Singapore).]

[14] CR 2007/23, 9 November 2007, p. 61, para. 27 (Jayakumar).

latter's first official visit to Singapore as Prime Minister. At this meeting they agreed that the dispute should be resolved through consultations on the basis of a formal exchange of documents.[15] However this exchange did not take place until much later.

Meeting between PM Goh Chok Tong and PM Dr Mahathir Mohamad (16 October 1991)

When Singapore Prime Minister Goh Chok Tong met Malaysian Prime Minister Dr Mahathir at the sidelines of the Commonwealth Heads of Government meeting (16 October 1991) in Harare, Zimbabwe, they discussed the publicity over the Pedra Branca issue. Dr Mahathir recalled he had agreed with Prime Minister Lee Kuan Yew in 1981 to exchange documents on Pedra Branca. Both of them had agreed that if the documents established that the island belonged to the other, both sides would accept that position. Prime Minister Goh mentioned our idea to have our documents made public but Dr Mahathir preferred to keep them out of the press.

Meeting between PM Goh Chok Tong and PM Dr Mahathir Mohamad (25 January 1992)

When Prime Minister Goh had a bilateral meeting with Dr Mahathir on 25 January 1992 at the sidelines of the 4th Association of Southeast Asian Nations (ASEAN) Summit held in Singapore, he reiterated the need to exchange documents so as to remove this bilateral irritant. At this meeting, Dr Mahathir agreed that both sides should exchange documents as soon as possible and that the two Attorneys General were to contact each other.

---

[15] Singapore's TPN SHC109/89, dated 1 July 1989, stated that in December 1981, Prime Minister Lee Kuan Yew and Prime Minister Dr Mahathir agreed that the two countries would exchange documents to establish each other's claim to Pedra Branca.

Meeting between PM Goh Chok Tong and Malaysian PM
Dr Mahathir Mohamad in Singapore (January 1992)
(Source: Ministry of Information, Communications and the Arts,
Singapore; Courtesy of National Archives of Singapore)

Dr Mahathir referred to this understanding at the press conference the next day. Dr Mahathir said that the question of who is the rightful owner of Pedra Branca should be determined through negotiations between the legal officials and based on legal documents. He also said that "Malaysia will stick to legal principles to settle the dispute." He added that "Malaysia had a lot of claims to make on several islands including Pulau Layang Layang, but it had to hold to one principle based on legality and not history." On 27 January 1992, *The Star* quoted him as saying: "*We have to hold to one principle ... we can't claim one island based on history and another using legal principle when it is to our convenience. I would like to stick to legal principle.*"[16]

---

[16] *The Star*, "Island row to be solved legally: Mahathir", 27 January 1992.

Why was there a Long Delay in the Formal Exchange of Documents?

The long delay in bringing about the exchange of documents was due mainly to three factors. First, bilateral relations between the two countries had deteriorated in the mid-eighties due to events such as the furore over the visit of Israeli President Chiam Herzog to Singapore in November 1986, then Second Minister for Defence Lee Hsien Loong's comments on Malays in the Singapore Armed Forces in April 1987 and Malaysia's allegation of the infringement of Malaysian sovereignty by four national servicemen from Singapore. Second, Dr Mahathir had other preoccupations with Malaysia's internal problems, including economic issues and leadership challenges within UMNO by Tun Musa Hitam (1986) and Tengku Razaleigh Hamzah (1988). Third, Malaysia in all likelihood did not have the documentary evidence needed to support its claim. The Secretary-General of Wisma Putra, Tan Sri Ahmad Kamil Jaafar told Singapore's Permanent Secretary of MFA, Peter Chan, in August 1990 that after they received the documents from Singapore, the Malaysians had sent a research team to London, India and Johor to look for documents on Pedra Branca.

Several Rounds of Bilateral Consultations

Within a few weeks after the meeting in January 1992 between the Prime Ministers, we followed up officially by sending to Malaysia our Memorandum and supporting documents.[17] After repeated reminders to them, Wisma Putra sent us Malaysia's own Memorandum in response on 29 June 1992.[18] Our legal experts immediately went about carefully examining the contents of the Malaysian Memorandum. As the Senior State Counsel,

---

[17] On 17 February 1992, under the cover of a letter from Singapore's Attorney-General dated 14 February 1992.

[18] This Memorandum was dated 20 June 1992.

Attorney-General's Chambers (AGC), Sivakant Tiwari, was away on a pilgrimage, the Deputy Secretary, MFA, Peter Ho, brought in Jeffrey Chan (who was Director of Legal Service, Ministry of Defence (MINDEF)) to help assess the Malaysian case. This is another illustration of the close working relationship between different agencies.

The exchange of documents was followed by two rounds of consultations, on 4–6 February 1993 and on 12–14 January 1994. In these consultations, the Malaysian team was led by Wisma Putra's Secretary-General, Kamil Jaafar, and the Singapore side by Tiwari, the principal officer in AGC on matters concerning international law. He was tasked to head the Inter-Ministry Committee on Pedra Branca, and was very familiar with the origins of the dispute and various issues in the case. Tiwari has an amiable personality but beneath that pleasant disposition was a tough and skilful negotiator. He was diplomatic and tactful and got along well with all our negotiating partners.

When Jayakumar asked Tiwari to describe these consultations, he responded:

> *"The First Round of Consultations was a very intense event – like a mini-trial. Each side presented its legal arguments and evidence. These were rebutted by the other side and further arguments were put forward with a promise that there could be supplementary rebuttals to follow after the end of the consultations.*
>
> *The Second Round of Consultations was just as intense as the first one – if not more so as each side had also to answer written arguments forwarded intersessionally. Apart from the arguments, the Second Round of Consultations was significant for three reasons.*
>
> *Firstly, Malaysia appeared to be concerned that Singapore should not spring a surprise on it in the future. Thus Kamil was very keen to know if Singapore had in fact presented every line of argument open to it.*
>
> *Secondly, Kamil mentioned the possibility of some "third party" being involved in the settlement of the dispute.*

It was not made clear whether this referred to a court or some other mode of settlement.

Thirdly, the Malaysians felt that the consultation process had been exhausted and indicated that the matter should be referred back to the two Prime Ministers for further guidance."

After the second round of consultations, Tiwari sent a note to inform MFA's Deputy Secretary, Peter Ho, saying that Kamil Jaafar had, for the first time, indicated that the issue may have to be presented before some third party as expressed by Singapore in our first Memorandum.[19] It was noteworthy that Kamil Jaafar did not expressly state the ICJ but left it as a "third party".

Later that year, on 6 September 1994, Prime Minister Goh and Dr Mahathir had yet another meeting in Langkawi. At the press conference following this meeting, Prime Minister Goh said that both sides had attempted to resolve the issue by exchanging documents, but "that was as far as the officials could go". He said that both he and Dr Mahathir decided in principle that the dispute should be referred to a third party such as the ICJ but would leave it to the officials to decide who the arbitrator should be.[20]

Shortly thereafter, on 17 September 1994, Malaysia sent a TPN agreeing to refer the Pedra Branca issue to the ICJ.

It therefore took some 14 years after the dispute arose, for the leaders of both countries to agree to resolve it through the ICJ. In fact, we had, on numerous occasions, from July 1989 onwards proposed in various TPNs that the matter be referred to third party adjudication and specifically proposed referring it to the ICJ.[21]

---

[19] Our Memorandum of February 1992, para. 5 mentioned the possibility of going to the ICJ.

[20] *The Straits Times*, "Pedra Branca issue goes to arbitration", 8 September 1994.

[21] The first TPN where we proposed the ICJ route was TPN SHC 109/89 dated 1 July 1989, which protested intrusions by Royal Malaysian Marine

One may ask: why did Malaysia persist in maintaining their claim even though, after studying our documents, their leaders and officials privately indicated that we had a strong case and their claim was weak? Firstly, it had become a sensitive political issue, especially in Johor. Since the matter had been politicised, it would probably have been untenable for any Malaysian leader to be seen making any territorial concession to Singapore. Secondly, the Malaysians could have subsequently sought the legal opinion of international Counsel, who might have advised them that they had a plausible, even a good, case.

Police vessels into Singapore territorial waters from 24 to 30 June 1989. The TPN referred to Foreign Minister Wong Kan Seng's statement during his meeting with his counterpart on 16 June 1989 and reiterated our offer that if the matter was not settled after the exchange of documents, "Singapore is prepared to have Malaysia's challenge to Singapore's ownership of Pedra Branca adjudicated upon by the International Court of Justice, whose decision shall be binding on both sides."

CHAPTER 4

NEGOTIATING THE SPECIAL AGREEMENT

Having reached a political decision to refer the dispute to the ICJ, the immediate task was for both sides to settle the terms of a "Special Agreement" to refer the case to the ICJ. This was necessary because neither Singapore nor Malaysia had filed a declaration accepting, in advance, the compulsory jurisdiction of the ICJ.[22] Therefore, the only way the Court could be vested with jurisdiction over the dispute was for both countries to sign a Special Agreement consenting to the Court hearing the case, and specifying the precise question the Court would be asked to decide.

Four Years to Settle the Special Agreement (1995–1998)

It took four years to work out the Special Agreement. Officials on both sides first met over three rounds of negotiations from 1995 to 1998 to settle the terms.[23] The Malaysian side was led by Kamil Jaafar, Secretary-General of the Malaysian Ministry of

---

[22] Article 36 (2) of the Statute of the ICJ.

[23] First Round: 15–16 June 1995, Kuala Lumpur; Second Round: 5–6 March 1996, Singapore; and Third Round: 14 April 1998, Kuala Lumpur.

Head of the Singapore delegation, Sivakant Tiwari, and
Head of the Malaysian delegation, Kamil Jaafar, exchanging the
Record of Meeting at the Malaysia-Singapore Senior Officials'
Meeting in Kuala Lumpur, June 1995 (Source: Bernama)

Foreign Affairs, in the first two rounds of negotiations. He had
retired by the time of the Third Round and was replaced by
Datuk Abdul Kadir Mohamed, the new Secretary-General of
Wisma Putra. Tiwari led the Singapore side in all three rounds.

Why did it take some four years to reach agreement on the
text of the Special Agreement? The delay was due to difficulties
in reaching agreement over three issues:

- Firstly, whether to list "Pedra Branca" or "Pulau Batu Puteh"
  first when describing the subject matter of the litigation;

- Secondly, whether the issue to be referred to the ICJ should
  also cover Middle Rocks and South Ledge. This was the
  most contentious of the three issues.

- Thirdly, whether to accept Malaysia's proposal to include a provision in the Agreement to the effect that if one side was adjudged to have sovereignty over Pedra Branca, the ICJ should also be asked to determine the rights or interests of the other party. Their objective was that the losing side should also be seen to get something.

(a) The Order of Listing: Pedra Branca or Pulau Batu Puteh

The Malaysians, at first, did not agree to the conventional alphabetical sequence of "Pedra Branca/Pulau Batu Puteh". They wanted the order reversed. It was only after much discussion that they agreed to go along with the conventional alphabetical sequence provided Singapore would agree to include the following additional text in the Special Agreement: "it being understood that the name Pedra Branca is synonymous with Pulau Batu Puteh". Kamil Jaafar's explanation for the proposed text was that the name "Pulau Batu Puteh" had existed all along and the Portuguese must have named it "Pedra Branca" or "White Rock" later.

Our Chief negotiator Tiwari did not accept this additional note as that could be interpreted to mean that historically the name "Pulau Batu Puteh" had preceded "Pedra Branca". Furthermore, the Malaysians could possibly use the expression to argue that since, from their viewpoint, Pulau Batu Puteh did not include Middle Rocks and South Ledge, Singapore had in effect conceded that the Special Agreement excluded Middle Rocks and South Ledge.

We remained deadlocked on this issue (as well as the issue of Middle Rocks and South Ledge). The breakthrough came only at the Third Round. Malaysia agreed to the conventional alphabetical sequence and the inclusion of Middle Rocks and South Ledge following agreement on a new Article 3 which stated, *inter alia*, that the order of the use of names would not be treated as having any relevance to the question of sovereignty to be determined by the ICJ.

(b) The Issue of Whether to Include Middle Rocks and South Ledge

Pedra Branca, Middle Rocks and South Ledge are located at the eastern entrance of the Singapore Strait. Like Pedra Branca, Middle Rocks are made of granite, and they are only 0.6 nautical miles from Pedra Branca. South Ledge lies 2.1 nautical miles to the south of Pedra Branca. It is also formed of granite and is a low-tide elevation. Both Middle Rocks and South Ledge are very small features. Malaysia first raised the issue of Middle Rocks and South Ledge at the first Malaysia-Singapore consultations on Pedra Branca in Kuala Lumpur from 4–6 February 1993. In his opening Statement, the Malaysian delegation leader, Kamil Jaafar, said that he used Middle Rocks and South Ledge as geographic references to Pedra Branca, stating that they were "two Malaysian islands south" of Pedra Branca. Tiwari disagreed pointing out that Middle Rocks and South Ledge were part of the same group as Pedra Branca and they were not part of Malaysian territory. Kamil Jaafar's rejoinder was that Middle Rocks and South Ledge fell within the area over which Johor possessed sovereignty prior to 1844.

At the next meeting, held in Singapore from 5–6 March 1996, the Malaysian delegation insisted that Middle Rocks and South Ledge belonged to Malaysia and that they had no mandate to discuss the reference of these two features to the ICJ. We maintained that we did not have the mandate to exclude Middle Rocks and South Ledge from the reference to the ICJ.

On 3 February 1997, then Malaysian Foreign Minister Abdullah Badawi wrote to then Foreign Minister Jayakumar "to resolve" the impasse over Middle Rocks and South Ledge. He referred to the various meetings between the Prime Ministers on both sides in December 1981, October 1991 and January 1992,

South Ledge at low tide, with two persons on the larger rock
(the wreck of MV Gichoon is to the right of the larger rock)
(Source: *Memorial of Singapore*, Case concerning Sovereignty over
Pedra Branca/Pulau Batu Puteh, Middle Rocks and South Ledge
(Malaysia/Singapore), Volume 1, Image 21).

and noted that these were focused solely on Pedra Branca. He
said Singapore had never mentioned Middle Rocks and South
Ledge as part of the dispute to be submitted to the ICJ.

During a golf game on 9 April 1997 in New Delhi,[24] Badawi
and Jayakumar discussed this matter. Jayakumar impressed on
Badawi that since the whole idea of going to the ICJ was to
resolve an outstanding territorial issue, then we should include
Middle Rocks and South Ledge; otherwise, we would still have
a residual problem.

On 5 May 1997, Jayakumar replied to Badawi reiterating
Singapore's understanding that Middle Rocks and South Ledge
were part of the dispute to be referred to the ICJ. In the letter,

[24] This was during an ASEAN Foreign Ministers golf game when both Foreign
Ministers were in India to attend the Non-Aligned Movement's ministerial
conference.

Jayakumar stated that "we shared the common objective that we should resolve the dispute over Pedra Branca in a conclusive and definitive manner". He further emphasised that "if Middle Rocks and South Ledge are not included in the reference to the ICJ, we will still have a residual unresolved territorial dispute".

The issue was finally resolved in April 1998, at the Third Round of meetings, when Malaysia acknowledged that there were three features involved (Pedra Branca, Middle Rocks and South Ledge).

(c) Flexibility over Territorial Rights and Interests of Losing Party

The Malaysians wanted some leeway in that the Court should also be asked to determine the rights and interests of the party not having sovereignty over Pedra Branca.

They wanted a scenario where if Malaysia had sovereignty over Pedra Branca, then Singapore could continue to operate the lighthouse; if Singapore got Pedra Branca, then Malaysian traditional fishing rights would continue. The Malaysians had earlier dropped hints that going to the ICJ need not be all or nothing. For example, their High Commissioner in Singapore Emam Haniff told our officials, MFA Deputy Secretary Peter Ho and Tiwari, separately on 15 June 1995 that it was about "face".

Then Permanent Secretary Kishore Mahbubani also reported on 6 June 1995 that, at an ASEAN-Senior Officials' Meeting, Kamil Jaafar told him that Malaysia would propose that if the International Court decided that Malaysia had sovereignty, they would allow Singapore to maintain the lighthouse there; if the Court decided that Singapore had sovereignty, Singapore should allow Malaysian fishermen to retain their traditional fishing rights around the island.

Likewise, Solicitor-General of Malaysia Heliliah bte Mohd Yusof told Tiwari on 31 March 1995 at a dinner in Kuala Lumpur that we should work out an arrangement whereby one country would own the island and the other country would have the right to use it.

It was clear from all these approaches that the Malaysians wanted a face saving way for both sides to emerge with something from the process.

On the surface, it seemed an innocuous, even reasonable proposal but we thought there were dangers in accepting it. We consulted our Counsel, one of whom cautioned us that if we went along with this Malaysian approach, it would be "allowing Malaysia a tactical advantage, in the sense that the Court may be tempted to take a middle way, if it is available". Another Counsel likewise warned us that it would invite the Court to arrive at "an 'equitable' decision by which Malaysia is accorded sovereignty on the basis of contiguity and Singapore is allowed to manage the lighthouse and use the landing pad".

Because there was a high risk that such a formulation would open the door to a middle way solution by the ICJ, we decided it would be most unwise for us to agree to Malaysia's proposal. As we did not agree, the Malaysians dropped this proposal.

With all three issues resolved, both sides finally agreed on the formulation and the text of the Agreement at the Third Round on 14 April 1998. Both parties also confirmed that the hearings would be held before the full Court (and not a chamber of the Court) and that each country would appoint a judge *ad hoc*.[25] The final agreed formulation of the question was:

> "The Court is requested to determine whether sovereignty over:
> (a) Pedra Branca/Pulau Batu Puteh;
> (b) Middle Rocks;
> (c) South Ledge;
> belongs to Malaysia or the Republic of Singapore."

Another Five Years to Sign and Ratify the Special Agreement (1998–2003)

One would have thought that the signing and ratification of the Agreement would follow expeditiously since the text had

---

[25] See "The Appointment of Judge *Ad Hoc*" in Chapter 5.

been agreed to by both sides. However, it took another five years before the Agreement was signed. There were two main reasons for this delay.

- Firstly, bilateral relations then were affected by spats over several issues, such as the release of Minister Mentor's memoirs, the relocation of Malaysia's Customs, Immigration and Quarantine (CIQ) at Tanjong Pagar, reclamation works by Singapore as well as the water issue. So both countries put the Pedra Branca issue on the back burner.
- Secondly, Malaysia also showed no real enthusiasm to sign the Special Agreement. We believed they wanted to see how they would fare in the case of Sipadan and Ligitan.

In fact, at a dinner he hosted on 14 April 1998, Wisma Putra Secretary-General Kadir commented to Tiwari that although the Special Agreement on Pedra Branca had been finalized, the Sipadan/Ligitan case involving Malaysia and Indonesia would have to be referred to the ICJ first, as the Special Agreement for that case had been signed before the Special Agreement on Pedra Branca.

It was only after the oral arguments at the ICJ on the Sipadan/Ligitan case had been completed (June 2002) that Malaysia began to show eagerness in getting the Special Agreement signed and ratified. They were probably encouraged by the oral hearings before the ICJ. As such, their confidence in winning the Sipadan/Ligitan case now spurred them to push for resolving the case with us on Pedra Branca. The Sipadan/Ligitan case was interesting in that Malaysia relied essentially on arguments based on *effectivites*[26] and not historical claim. It was ironic

---

[26] A term describing acts of State administration or exercise of State authority which may be taken as evidence of sovereignty or territorial jurisdiction. This may include enacting legislation, controlling access or generally exercising police power. In the Sipadan/Ligitan case, the main *effectivites* relied on by Malaysia were enacting legislation to turn the islands into bird sanctuaries, regulating the collection of turtle eggs and constructing a light beacon without seeking Indonesia's permission.

that in the Pedra Branca case, Malaysia was unable to present any evidence whatsoever of its *effectivites* with regard to Pedra Branca and its claim essentially turned on possession of original title. On the other hand, we were able to present an impressive array of *effectivites* both by Britain and Singapore.

During the second half of 2002, Malaysia suggested that the Special Agreement could be signed on dates coinciding with scheduled talks on the water issue in late November 2002. Those talks, however, were called off by Malaysia. On 3 January 2003, we proposed that the signing take place at the sidelines of the ASEAN–EU Ministerial meeting in Brussels (27–28 January 2003), but Malaysia did not agree to that. Meanwhile, Malaysia continued to give great play in their media to a claim that Singapore was dragging its feet on bringing the case to the ICJ.

Finally, it was settled that both sides would sign the Agreement on 6 February 2003 in Kuala Lumpur. Singapore followed up almost immediately by ratifying the Agreement on 15 February 2003. But unaccountably, it took Malaysia some three months before they ratified the Agreement on 17 May 2003.

Both sides exchanged instruments of ratification on 9 May 2003 through diplomatic channels. The joint notification to the Registrar of the ICJ, which was signed by both foreign ministers, was submitted by the co-agents of the governments of Singapore and Malaysia on 24 July 2003.

CHAPTER 5

PREPARING FOR THE ICJ HEARINGS

O nce it was settled that the case was to be submitted to the ICJ, we had to get started at once on a great deal of preparatory work. Actually, AGC had already done a lot of background work between 1992 and 2003. This phase required very close cooperation and coordination among different agencies, each of which had useful special inputs or possible access to key documents unavailable at AGC or at MFA.

Getting a Good Inter-Agency Team

It may be recalled that Malaysia first agreed to refer the dispute to the ICJ on 17 September 1994. A few days later, on 21 September 1994, Jayakumar sent a note to Attorney-General on the need to put together a first rate inter-agency team. He wrote:

> *"The IMC should consider setting up a task force which will assemble some of our best legal resources. This task force should work on this issue from now on right up to the time the ICJ has handed its ruling. (It will take several years.) AG's Chambers alone does not have the resources. Therefore, consider harnessing the best people from the NUS law faculty, MINDEF legal services and even some of the best brains among the advocates and solicitors."*

Members of the AGC Team (Front row, from left: Pang Khang Chau,
Sivakant Tiwari, Daren Tang. Back row, from left: Tan Ken Hwee,
Ong Chin Heng, Bek Ching Ching, Lionel Yee)
(Source: Tan Ken Hwee)

Fortunately, we had set up the Inter-Ministry Committee
on Pedra Branca ("IMC on Pedra Branca") prior to 1989 that
included officials from AGC, MFA, MINDEF, Ministry of Law,
Ministry of Communications (now Ministry of Transport), Port of
Singapore Authority (PSA) (now the Maritime and Port Authority
of Singapore (MPA)) and the Oral History Department.

The IMC started gathering our documents and materials
through the different agencies represented. The most significant
of the many documents we located was the Acting State Secretary
of Johor's 1953 letter expressly disclaiming title to Pedra
Branca. We found this document during one of our earliest
searches, which started after we had the first intimations that
the Malaysians were making inquiries about Pedra Branca. In
1977, the then Ministry of Communications had located in its

archives a set of correspondence from the office of the Colonial Secretary related to Pedra Branca that included this 1953 letter.

Tiwari had also arranged for the National Archives to examine the microfilm of documents that Jayakumar brought back from London in 1978. Separately, he had arranged for the two surviving Light Housekeepers (Cyril Spencer Galistan and Henry Nunes) to be interviewed by the Oral History Department as they were getting on in age.

After Malaysia agreed to refer the case to the ICJ, it was internally agreed that AGC would be responsible for preparing the Singapore Government's case. Thereafter, the Attorney-General set up a Task Force in AGC chaired by Tiwari to work on the legal case whilst the IMC would continue to attend to the collection of evidence and other co-ordination work. Yeo Bock Chuan and Tan Ken Hwee (then doing national service in the Legal Department of MINDEF) were co-opted into the AGC Legal Team. Other Legal Officers joined the Task Force at different times when they were posted to the Chambers. This Task Force continued its work right up till the hearings of the Pedra Branca case.

To augment the work of the IMC, an Executive group was formed in 2003 under Second Permanent Secretary for Foreign Affairs, Bilahari Kausikan to have oversight and manage the ground situation in the vicinity of Pedra Branca. The purpose of this group was to ensure that actions taken by various agencies were consistent with our position and sovereignty of Pedra Branca. Of particular concern was a marked increase in the number of intrusions of Malaysian Government vessels in the waters around Pedra Branca. For example, from the period 1990–2000, there were some 64 incidents. However, in the next eight years from the period 2000–2008, there were a total of 563 recorded intrusions with the highest recorded number of incidents (167) in 2007 alone.

These Malaysian actions did not make any sense to us because the Court would take into account only the conduct and activities of both sides prior to the critical date. Actions on the ground after the case had been referred to the Court could not help to strengthen the case for either side. We took note of these intrusions and regularly recorded our protests, where we would say:

> *"These actions are not consistent with the agreement between our respective Governments to refer the issue of Pedra Branca to the International Court of Justice (ICJ) for peaceful settlement. The Singapore Government seeks the co-operation of the Malaysian Government to ensure the immediate cessation of incidents of this nature. The Singapore Government wishes to point out that no number of actions on the part of Malaysian Government vessels will affect the ICJ's determination of this dispute."*

Visiting Pedra Branca for First Hand Look

As part of the preparations, we arranged for key members of the team to visit Pedra Branca to get a first hand look and feel of the island. It was necessary to see for oneself the subject matter of the dispute.

Chief Justice Chan Sek Keong (when he was Attorney-General) visited Pedra Branca on 16 August 1994. He was accompanied by Tiwari and other officials. Our international Counsel also made a special effort to visit the island on 18 March 1996, when they were in Singapore for meetings with the team. Before the oral pleadings, Tommy Koh visited the island with members of the inter-agency team on 6 July 2007. This time, the party travelled by helicopter so that the team members would not get sea-sick!

Many years earlier, on 15 October 1988, Jayakumar had made his own visit to Pedra Branca with the Minister for Communications and Information, Yeo Ning Hong. It was planned as an overnight trip as Jayakumar, an avid fisherman, also hoped to fish the following morning. They travelled by sea on the old but sturdy PSA vessel, the *Mata Ikan*. After a delicious curry dinner on the boat, a huge storm erupted with

Sivakant Tiwari and Chan Sek Keong with Coast guard officers during a visit to Pedra Branca in 1994 (Source: Sivakant Tiwari)

little warning. The winds were so ferocious that the ropes securing their lifeboat snapped and most of the crockery carried on board was smashed! Fortunately, the crew was very experienced and they rode out the enormous waves in pitch darkness for two hours. Sadly, two men on a fishing boat from Punggol, whom they had greeted earlier in the evening, died in that storm.

Assembling a Team of Good International Counsel

It was also important for us to assemble a team of good international Counsel. Up to this point, all of the legal research had been done by AGC, but with the decision to go to the ICJ we needed the services of top international lawyers. This was necessary because international Counsel who had previously argued many cases before the Court would be thoroughly familiar with the workings and procedures of the Court. Moreover, they would be experts in international law. Therefore, soon

International Counsel (From left: Alain Pellet, Ian Sinclair,
Thomas Franck and Ian Brownlie) with Sivakant Tiwari during a
visit to Pedra Branca in 1996 (Source: Tan Ken Hwee)[27]

Tommy Koh with Tan Kim Siew in a helicopter on a visit to
Pedra Branca in 2007 (Source: Ministry of Foreign Affairs, Singapore)

---

[27] Sir Ian Sinclair QC and Professor Thomas Franck had advised us in earlier
stages of our case.

Before the storm: Yeo Ning Hong, Jayakumar and Goon Kok Loon
aboard the Mata Ikan during a visit to Pedra Branca in 1988
(Source: Maritime and Port Authority of Singapore)

after Kamil Jaafar intimated to Tiwari (on 17 January 1994) that Malaysia might agree to the third party route, Jayakumar asked Tiwari to attend to this urgently and put up names for consideration by the government. Tiwari put up his first list of possible international Counsel on 15 February 1994. A fuller account of our international Counsel is set out in Chapter 7 of this book.

The Appointment of Judge *Ad Hoc*

Under the Statutes of the ICJ where a State appearing as a party in a case does not have its national on the ICJ bench, it is entitled to appoint a judge *ad hoc*.[28] A judge *ad hoc* serves as a member of the Court for a specific case. Since neither Malaysia nor Singapore had its national on the Court, each was entitled to appoint a judge *ad hoc*.

Tommy Koh was our Initial Choice

The team initially decided that Tommy Koh should be Singapore's judge *ad hoc*. Within Government, it was thought that he would be an excellent choice as he had wide international diplomatic experience. He was well known in international circles and was highly regarded especially for the excellent way he had presided over the closing stages of the Third United Nations Conference on the Law of the Sea. Some of our international Counsel also agreed that Tommy was a very good choice. Tommy was already involved as part of the team preparing for the case, and no one on the Singapore side anticipated that this fact may prove to be an obstacle to nominating him as judge *ad hoc*.

A problem, however, did arise. On 2 October 1995, Tommy informed Jayakumar that at the first meeting of the international Counsel, our French Counsel, Professor Alain Pellet, expressed reservations about Tommy being our judge *ad hoc*. He argued that his appointment might give rise to objections since he had

---

[28] Article 31 of the Statute of the ICJ.

been involved in our preparation of the case. Pellet had in mind Article 17 of the ICJ Statute which stated:

> *"(1)   No member of the Court may act as agent, counsel, or advocate in any case.*
>
> *(2)   No member may participate in the decision of any case in which he has previously taken part as agent, counsel, or advocate for one of the parties, or as a member of a national or international court, or of a commission of enquiry, or in any other capacity.*
>
> *(3)   Any doubt on this point shall be settled by the decision of the Court."*

Although Tommy at that point had not been appointed Agent and was not our counsel, the question was whether the words "… taken part … in any other capacity" would disqualify him. The only way to avoid any such complication was for Tommy to withdraw immediately from our team and not to be involved any further in our internal preparations for the case.

This complication caused some dismay amongst the Singapore team. Jayakumar, Tommy and Attorney-General Chan Sek Keong discussed what would be the best course of action. They agreed that the team should take time to reflect on the matter and not make a hasty decision. The question they asked was: how could Tommy best serve Singapore's interests — as judge *ad hoc* or as a key member of the Singapore team which would prepare our case and make the arguments before the Court?

While the other international Counsel did not seem as exercised over this issue as Pellet was, we asked Attorney-General to do further research on the legal practice and precedents of the Court, and to assess whether the concerns expressed by Pellet were well founded.

The research proved inconclusive but showed that there was no absolute prohibition in such a situation. After weighing all the considerations, the Singapore Government decided to rule out Tommy as judge *ad hoc*. The main consideration was that it was not worth running the risk of having Malaysia object to

Tommy's appointment. In that event, the Court would have to rule on the issue and if it should uphold Malaysia's objection it would mean that we would have started off with the Court on a wrong footing. We would then have to appoint another judge *ad hoc* and both he and the Court would know that he was not our first choice.

We Settled on Judge Rao as our Judge *Ad Hoc*

We therefore had to come up with other names for judge *ad hoc*. We concluded that there was no one else within Singapore with the same credentials as Tommy for this position. We evaluated a few well known foreign lawyers and we consulted our international Counsel. A major consideration was that the judge *ad hoc* should ideally be a person familiar with British colonial history and the structure, functions and practices of the British colonial civil service during the relevant period. A large part of the evidence in the case concerned acts of the British authorities during the colonial era, including the period when Singapore was under the governance of the East India Company. After careful consideration and after consulting our international Counsel, we decided on P S Rao. Rao had been much involved in issues relating to the Law of the Sea, and had represented India during the negotiations on the UN Convention of the Law of the Sea. He was also a member of the International Law Commission. Our international Counsel Pellet sounded out Rao informally regarding the appointment as judge *ad hoc* and Rao agreed.

Chan Sek Keong is Appointed Chief Justice and Chao Hick Tin Becomes the New Attorney-General — Should the New Chief Justice Continue to be Involved in the Case?

When Chan Sek Keong became Attorney-General on 1 May 1992, preparations for the Pedra Branca case were already underway. Before his appointment as Attorney-General, he had been a Judicial Commissioner and later Judge of the Supreme Court for six years. Chan Sek Keong, together with Tommy Koh, was in the first batch of local law graduates. After graduation he practised law for more than 24 years before being appointed to the Judiciary.

Chan Sek Keong brought to the team his valuable perspectives as an advocate, a Judge and an Attorney-General. He immediately plunged himself into the Pedra Branca case and very quickly acquainted himself thoroughly with all aspects of the case — both the legal issues as well as tactical considerations. He took charge of the preparations for the case and directed the AGC team. He also chaired all meetings with the international Counsel. Chan Sek Keong had a deep interest in the history of Malaya and the Straits Settlements, and this knowledge proved most useful because the historical aspects of the case were an important part of the case. Indeed, he even brought books from his personal library to The Hague!

On 11 April 2006, Chan Sek Keong was appointed Chief Justice and former Judge of Appeal, Judge Chao Hick Tin, was appointed Attorney-General. We were happy to have Chao Hick Tin in the Pedra Branca team. Before becoming a Judge, he had served in AGC and had headed its Civil Division. He had worked closely with Jayakumar, Tommy Koh and Tiwari in the UN Conference on the Law of the Sea negotiations. He had maintained a keen interest in international law and was familiar with the legal issues of the case.

With Chan Sek Keong's appointment as Chief Justice, we had to address the question of whether he should remain involved with the preparations of the case. More importantly, should he be a member of the team that would argue the case at The Hague? This was a critical time as we knew that the oral hearings would take place within a year.

It would obviously have been a major loss if, at this critical juncture, Chan Sek Keong was completely cut off from any further work on the case or ceased to be part of our team appearing at

The Hague. Within the Singapore team of officials there were divergent views. While all acknowledged that Chan Sek Keong had done an excellent job in steering the preparations, some were concerned that inclusion of the Chief Justice in our team in The Hague might raise eyebrows as it was unusual for the Chief Justice of any state to plead before the ICJ. For example, would it blur the distinctions between the executive and the judiciary? Would foreign critics who attack the independence of our Judiciary use this as an additional argument? Jayakumar discussed with those who had expressed disquiet and posed to them these considerations: what was our most important objective? Based on this objective, would Chief Justice's inclusion be a "plus" or "minus"? All agreed that the most important objective was to ensure that we had the best talent to win the case, and that it was in our interest to have Chan Sek Keong continue his work on the case.

We also brainstormed this issue with international Counsel. They commented that it was unprecedented for a serving Chief Justice to argue in the oral hearings, but they had no strong views one way or the other. They said that the decision was really up to Chief Justice and the Government.

Jayakumar then discussed this with Chan Sek Keong to ascertain if he had any qualms. He had none. This matter was also discussed with Prime Minister Lee Hsien Loong and Minister Mentor Lee Kuan Yew and other Cabinet colleagues, and ultimately we had no doubts that Chan Sek Keong would be an asset to the team and that there was nothing improper about the Chief Justice leading our team to The Hague. We decided that we should be upfront and publicly mention Chief Justice's continuing role. In his statement in Parliament on 3 April 2006 concerning changes to the legal service as well as the appointment of a new Chief Justice and a new Attorney-General, Jayakumar said the following:

> *"Sir, as Minister for Law, I have observed first hand the high quality of Mr Chan Sek Keong's contributions. For instance, I was present in Hamburg during the hearings*

of the International Tribunal on the Law of the Sea in the case brought against us by Malaysia concerning reclamation within our territorial waters. He and his team did Singapore proud in ably presenting our legal arguments before that Tribunal. I should add that he has been playing a pivotal role in overseeing our preparations for the case we have with Malaysia on Pedra Branca before the International Court of Justice (ICJ). I am grateful to him for agreeing to continue with this role until the ICJ has heard and decided that case."[29]

In the oral hearings, in his opening statement, Tommy Koh made it a point to explain to the ICJ Judges Chief Justice Chan Sek Keong's role:

"I would like now to explain the presence of the Chief Justice of Singapore in our delegation. Mr Chan Sek Keong was Singapore's Attorney-General for 14 years, a position he relinquished in April last year when he was appointed as the Chief Justice of Singapore. He became involved in this case beginning in 1993, with the first series of bilateral consultations between Singapore and Malaysia. After the Special Agreement was submitted to this Court, Mr Chan led the legal team in preparing our written pleadings. In view of the pivotal role which he has played in overseeing Singapore's preparations for this case, when he was appointed Chief Justice, the Singapore Parliament was informed that he had agreed, at the Government's request, to continue with this role until the case has been decided by this Court."[30]

Close Coordination between Chan Sek Keong, Tommy Koh, Chao Hick Tin and Jayakumar

Although they had scheduled working meetings with the international Counsel, Chan Sek Keong, Tommy Koh and

---

[29] Parliamentary Debates Singapore, Vol. 81, Column 1723 (3 April 2006).

[30] CR 2007/20, 6 November 2007, p. 17, para. 6 (Koh).

Tommy Koh, Jayakumar, Chan Sek Keong and Chao Hick Tin at
the Great Hall of Justice, Peace Palace (Source: Ministry of
Foreign Affairs, Singapore)

Jayakumar also met over lunch every three or four months to
review developments and assess the progress of work being done.
The lunches were useful in enabling them to review developments,
to discuss questions and issues that had arisen, and to agree
on a common approach to the work. They did this over a few
years when the written pleadings were being prepared. When
Chan Sek Keong became Chief Justice, they continued with this
practice, and the new Attorney-General, Chao Hick Tin, also
joined these lunches.

Chan Sek Keong, Tommy and Jayakumar had known each
other for a long time and were contemporaries at law school.
Chao Hick Tin had worked with Tommy and Jayakumar at the
UNCLOS meetings, and was also a close friend. Their personal
relationship and mutual respect for each other was an important
factor for the effective functioning of the team.

The Involvement and Support from Prime Ministers and Cabinet

Throughout the span of nearly three decades, each of the three Prime Ministers — Lee Kuan Yew, Goh Chok Tong and Lee Hsien Loong — took a deep interest in the management of the dispute as well as in the preparations of the case at the ICJ.

All three Prime Ministers left it to the team to prepare the case. They showed full confidence in the team and did not attempt to micro-manage.

Lee Kuan Yew, who was Prime Minister when the dispute arose, deserves special mention. He paid attention not only to the political and diplomatic aspects, but also to the legal issues. Being a lawyer himself, he posed searching questions on the strength of our case and made helpful suggestions on legal arguments and tactics. For example, in the early days he felt that we should let Malaysia know that we had a good legal case. In the later stages, when he was Minister Mentor, Lee Kuan Yew remained deeply interested in the case.

Over the years, Jayakumar as Minister for Law, kept the Prime Minister and Cabinet posted on key developments and, where necessary, sought Cabinet's approval. These included questions relating to Middle Rock and South Ledge, the appointment of the judge *ad hoc* and appointment of an Agent.

A few weeks before departing from Singapore for The Hague for the oral hearings, the team gave a full briefing to Prime Minister Lee Hsien Loong and his Cabinet. The briefing covered the key planks of our case and Malaysia's case. Prime Minister and Cabinet were satisfied with the briefing. They commented that we had done the best we could in preparing a strong case and wished the team good luck.

CHAPTER 6

THE WRITTEN PLEADINGS

Proceedings before the ICJ are divided into written and oral phases. For the written phase, Malaysia and Singapore agreed to exchange three rounds of written pleadings under the Special Agreement signed by them, namely, the Memorial, the Counter-Memorial and the Reply.[31] Both sides agreed to submit the Memorial on 25 March 2004, the Counter-Memorial on 25 January 2005 and the Reply on 25 November 2005. They further agreed that there was no need for a fourth round of written pleadings. The whole process would take nearly three years.

Simultaneous Submission of Pleadings

Since the case was jointly submitted to the ICJ by Special Agreement, neither country was or could be considered a claimant or a respondent. The two parties were on an equal footing and each party was obliged to make out its claim to ownership of Pedra Branca. In view of this, the Special Agreement stipulated

---

[31] Under the Special Agreement, we agreed to exchange: (i) a Memorial within eight months; (ii) a Counter-Memorial, not later than ten months from the date of receipt of the Memorial; and (iii) a Reply, not later than ten months from the date of receipt of the Counter-Memorial.

that the written pleadings would be submitted simultaneously and not consecutively. If the two sides had agreed to submit their pleadings consecutively, they could probably have saved one round of written pleadings. In 2006, the ICJ issued a new practice direction discouraging the practice of simultaneous deposit of pleadings in cases brought by Special Agreement.

Research and Preparation

Putting together the written pleadings required extensive preparation, research, consultation, drafting and consensus-making. Considering that we had to produce three rounds of written pleadings, the process required many helping hands.

The process of research and the preparation of our case picked up pace once the Prime Ministers of Malaysia and Singapore agreed, in 1994, to refer the dispute to the ICJ. The process was multi-tiered and inclusive. We consulted local and international experts on international law and Malay history.[32]

At the next level, we constituted an inter-ministry committee chaired by Tiwari to plan and co-ordinate the whole effort systematically with the involvement of all key Ministries and agencies. In addition to AGC, the committee included representatives of MFA, MINDEF, MPA and the National Archives of Singapore (NAS). NAS made a major contribution and we would therefore like to elaborate on its role.

Role of NAS

We suspect that very few Singaporeans know what NAS does and fewer still have visited its premises and gallery at 1 Canning Rise or used its online sources. The NAS is the custodian of

---

[32] We consulted Associate Professor Robert Beckman, Associate Professor Ernest Chew, Associate Professor Edwin Lee, Kwa Chong Guan and Emeritus Professor Mary Turnbull.

our nation's official records and collective memory. In the case of Pedra Branca, it was enlisted to help us with our extensive research, both in our own archives and in foreign archives. One of our international Counsel, Ian Brownlie, remarked to a member of our team at The Hague that he would not have been able to write his written and oral pleadings without the materials provided to him by NAS and AGC.

The NAS started its research on Pedra Branca and related issues in the 1970s. In the early years, its main task was to do an inventory of the archival materials, fill in gaps by acquiring materials from other archives and nurture its relationships with Indian, Dutch and other national archives. From 2003 to 2006, NAS was officially included in the process of preparation and became an active partner in the information race. With a grant of $1.38 million from MFA, NAS adopted a two-prong strategy. First, NAS deployed five full-time staff[33] and ten part-timers[34] to conduct research. They were tasked to locate archival records and documents relating to the collection of lighthouse dues, maps and hydrographic surveys of the areas around Pedra Branca, British practices in taking possession of territories, the Straits Lights System, acts of piracy, the Malay concept of sovereignty, the role of British advisers and the status of the Sultan of Johore. In total, NAS staff spent over 20,000 research hours, identified more than 2,000 records, and transcribed 650 historical manuscripts for AGC.

NAS also engaged the services of a number of foreign researchers to assist us in acquiring copies of archival records from the archival depositories of the UK, India, Indonesia, Netherlands, Australia and New Zealand. From the UK, NAS secured the assistance of Dr Susan Sutton and Justine Taylor, and from Australia of Dr Brian Wimborne. Dr Julianti Parani

---

[33] Elaine Goh, Ng Yoke Lin, Ang-Low Kia Hiang, Stanley Tan and Yvonne Chan.

[34] Lim Guan Hock, France Goh, Joanne Yip, Mok Ly Yng, Jessie Tng, among others.

Team from the National Archives of Singapore (From left: Paul Chan,
Ang-Low Kia Hiang, Jessie Thng, Kevin Khoo, Elaine Goh,
Yvonne Chan, Pitt Kuan Wah, Stanley Tan, Ng Yoke Lin)
(Source: National Archives of Singapore)

assisted NAS in Indonesia. In the Netherlands and India, the
staff from their national archives assisted NAS.

In 2007, NAS staff were on standby during the entire
course of the oral proceedings on the Pedra Branca case at
the ICJ to assist the Singapore team at The Hague. NAS also
assisted AGC after the oral proceedings, in answering the
two questions posed by Judge Kenneth Keith of the ICJ. NAS
was able to locate new records and to review the records that
had been previously submitted to AGC. NAS deployed a total
of 11 full-time and 3 part-time staff to work on the Pedra
Branca case.

NAS Role Indispensable

It is fair to say that without the help of NAS, AGC and international Counsel would not have the materials with which to write the written or oral pleadings. What gems did NAS uncover which were found extremely useful by the team? One was a letter written by the Dutch colonial authority in Indonesia acknowledging that Pedra Branca was "British territory", which we used as evidence to support our case. The other was the 1925 letter from Sultan Abdul Rahman to Sultan Hussein that formally divided the Johor-Riau-Lingga Sultanate into two parts.

A Committee of Peers

AGC was given primary responsibility for overseeing the preparation of the written pleadings. The AGC team was led by the current Chief Justice, Chan Sek Keong, and included Tiwari, Pang Khang Chau, Tan Ken Hwee, Lionel Yee and Daren Tang. The drafting committee, chaired by Chan Sek Keong, included Jayakumar, Tommy Koh and our four international Counsel. Our history consultant, Mary Turnbull, attended some of the meetings of the drafting committee.

How did the drafting committee work? All the meetings of the committee were chaired by Chan Sek Keong. The first drafts of the various chapters of our Memorial were done either by the AGC team or the international Counsel to whom the particular topic and chapter had been allocated. The committee then met to go over the draft very carefully, paragraph by paragraph, discussing both substance and form. We debated our differences of opinion until a consensus was reached. The dynamics in the committee were that of a committee of peers, without any distinction between the Singaporean and foreign members. The Singapore members did not hesitate to challenge the international Counsel and the whole process was intellectually robust but collegial and good-humoured.

In preparing the Memorial, the drafting committee met three times: (i) in Paris on 9 and 10 March 2003; (ii) in London on 10 and 11 June 2003; and (iii) in Singapore on 27 and 28 October 2003. After the third meeting, the text of the Memorial was finalized and set in proper format, with all the footnotes checked and the six volumes of Annexes prepared. On 20 January 2004, AGC sent the Memorial for printing. The printer, SNP International Publishing Pte Ltd, did a very good job for us.

Sending the Memorial to the ICJ

We sent the Memorial (125 copies for the ICJ Registry and 20 copies for Malaysia) as diplomatic cargo, accompanied by a courier, to our Embassy in Brussels in March 2004. On 25 March 2004, all the copies of the Memorial were transported by land from Brussels to The Hague and safely delivered to the Registrar of the ICJ and to the Malaysian Embassy. Our Co-Agent, Ambassador Walter Woon (now Attorney-General), attended to the submission of the Memorial personally.[35] For our Counter-Memorial and Reply, Malaysia and Singapore subsequently decided to exchange the extra 20 copies in Kuala Lumpur and Singapore in order to save time. However, 125 copies of the Counter-Memorial and Reply still had to be delivered to the ICJ Registry. Why does the ICJ need so many copies? The Registrar gives copies of the pleadings to the Judges, to the opposite Party, keeps some in the Registry, and some in reserve in case a third State or States seek to intervene. Once the oral proceedings begin, the written pleadings were made available to the public and the press in the ICJ's library in the International Press Centre of The Hague, and in the UN's libraries and information centres around the world. Unlike an arbitration, the process of adjudication before the ICJ is transparent and accessible to the public and the press.

---

[35] Singapore's Attorneys General who were involved in the Pedra Branca case: Tan Boon Teik (1 January 1969–30 April 1992), Chan Sek Keong (1 May 1992–10 April 2006), Chao Hick Tin (11 April 2006–11 April 2008) and Walter Woon (11 April 2008–present).

Preparing the Counter-Memorial and Reply

After the Singapore team received the Malaysian Memorial, copies were given to each member of the team. After reading the Memorial, we each conveyed our preliminary observations to Chan Sek Keong. The AGC team then met to analyse and study these comments before sending our final comments on each section of the Memorial to our international Counsel. The whole team then met in London on 9 and 10 May 2004 to exchange views and to decide on our strategy for drafting our Counter-Memorial. Drafts were prepared and discussed at another meeting in London on 26 and 27 July 2004. A final meeting was held in Singapore on 30 September and 1 October 2004. The Counter-Memorial was delivered to the Registrar of the ICJ and to Malaysia on 25 January 2005.

The same process was repeated in the preparation of the Reply. The drafting committee assembled in London, on 2 March 2005, to discuss Malaysia's Counter-Memorial and to agree on a strategy for preparing our Reply. Jayakumar suggested that it would be useful to get someone who had not been closely involved in the preparations to comment on the pleadings of both sides. It would be good, before we finalised the Reply, to have such an independent and neutral view. Tommy and Chan Sek Keong agreed. Jayakumar then approached one of Singapore's prominent lawyers, Senior Counsel Davinder Singh and sent him the pleadings of both sides. We were encouraged by his opinion and response:

> *"The Memorials which have been submitted by Singapore are highly impressive and extremely well researched and presented. Singapore has the better argument .... The focus of our Memorials has rightly been on the law and its application to the facts. Our Memorials come across as comprehensive, intellectually honest, analytical, logical and legally sound."*

The committee met again in London on 22 and 23 May 2005 and in Singapore on 11 and 12 August 2005. The Reply

Copies of our written pleadings
(Source: Ministry of Foreign Affairs, Singapore)

was delivered to the ICJ and Malaysia on 25 November 2005. The committee requested that the Singapore Agent talk to the Malaysia Agent to confirm that the two sides wished to conclude the written proceedings with the Reply and to ask the ICJ for early dates for the oral hearing.

The Written Pleadings of Singapore and Malaysia

What were the main arguments contained in Singapore's pleadings? They were:

- Pedra Branca was *terra nullius* or no man's land in 1847;
- In 1847–1851, the British took possession of Pedra Branca to build Horsburgh Lighthouse;
- The British took possession of Pedra Branca without seeking permission from any other power;
- The British acquired sovereignty over Pedra Branca during 1847–1851;

- This sovereignty was maintained continuously for more than 150 years through continuous administration of Pedra Branca and the waters around it; and

- Malaysia had:

  (a) acquiesced in Britain's and later Singapore's sovereignty;

  (b) expressly recognised Singapore's sovereignty; and

  (c) unconditionally disclaimed title to the island.

What were the main arguments contained in the Malaysian pleadings? They were:

- Pedra Branca was not *terra nullius*;

- Malaysia had original title to Pedra Branca dating from the Johor-Riau-Lingga Sultanate in the 16th century;

- The British had sought and obtained permission to build Horsburgh Lighthouse on Pedra Branca from the Sultan of Johor;

- The British had never sought to establish sovereignty on Pedra Branca but were only a lighthouse operator; and

- Singapore had never publicly asserted sovereignty over Pedra Branca until 1979.

With the completion of the written pleadings, it was possible to identify the following issues and questions as the main areas of differences between the two Parties:

- Was Pedra Branca *terra nullius* in 1847?

- Did Johor have original title to Pedra Branca?

- Did the British intend to acquire sovereignty over Pedra Branca?

- Did the British seek and obtain permission to build the Horsburgh Lighthouse from Johor?

- Did Malaysia acquiesce in the British, and later, Singapore's sovereignty over Pedra Branca?

- If the title was indeterminate in 1847–1851, which of the two Parties had stronger *effectivites* or activities carried out as the sovereign?

Comments on Malaysia's Written Pleadings

After reading the Malaysian written pleadings, we formed several impressions, both favourable and unfavourable. First, we were relieved that they did not contain a smoking gun, that is, the missing 1844 letter from Governor Butterworth to the Sultan and Temenggong of Johore. We had in our possession copies of the replies of the Sultan and the Temenggong to Governor Butterworth. It was clear from the replies that Governor Butterworth had written to the Sultan and the Temenggong for permission to build a lighthouse on a nearby island off the coast of Johor. But without a copy of the original letter, we could not be sure which island Governor Butterworth was referring to.

The Singapore view of the Temenggong's reply, was that the British had selected Peak Rock as the location for the lighthouse. However, the Malaysians alleged that it must have been or was referable to Pedra Branca. Because of its critical importance, the Singapore team had made strenuous efforts to search for the document in both the archives in London and in India, but to no avail. We were therefore quite disappointed and indeed outraged that Malaysia, on the first day of their first round of pleadings at the ICJ, insinuated that we had deliberately concealed this letter.

Second, we thought that their pleadings had been cleverly crafted and gave Malaysia's case a seemingly attractive appearance. Third, we thought that Malaysia's arguments on historic title were not very convincing. Chan Sek Keong, who had immersed himself in Malayan history, was confident that he could rebut or weaken the Malaysian case on historic title sufficiently for the Court to hold that Malaysia had failed to prove such claim.

Fourth, we wondered why Malaysia had wasted so much time, effort and paper on lighthouses in general and the Straits Lights

System, in particular.[36] We did not disagree with Malaysia on this point. Some lighthouses are built on territory which belongs to the operator of the lighthouse. Other lighthouses are built on territory which belongs to a foreign sovereign. Horsburgh Lighthouse is built on Pedra Branca which belongs to Singapore. The lighthouse on Pulau Pisang, although operated by Singapore, is built on land which belongs to Johor. Therefore, the legal status of Pedra Branca is clearly distinguishable from the legal status of Pulau Pisang. Malaysia's attempt to treat Singapore's administration of the two lighthouses as having the same legal consequence in international law was obviously wrong.

Fifth, we were not impressed by the affidavit of Malaysia's retired Commodore, Thanabalasingam, and basically decided to ignore it. Commodore Thanabalasingam had filed an affidavit stating that, prior to the critical date, he had advised his own Government that Pedra Branca belonged to Malaysia and also he had landed on Pedra Branca in the firm belief that it belonged to Malaysia. Since it was an internal communication and not in the public domain, it had no probative value. Malaysia brought him to The Hague and there was speculation that they may offer him as a witness, but we decided that in that event we will decline to cross-examine him.

Sixth, we were disappointed by the manner in which Malaysia had dealt with our pleadings, e.g., using partial quotations and distorting our arguments. This was unfortunately a forerunner of Malaysia's attitude and tactics during the oral proceedings.

Who Won the Written Pleadings?

The first stage of the battle was fought by way of written pleadings. Who won the battle? We did not know, but the

---

[36] Malaysia had devoted a large part of its Counter-Memorial in arguing that building or operating a lighthouse is not indicative of sovereignty over the territory on which the lighthouse stands.

Singapore team felt comfortable with our pleadings. We, of course, did not know what the judges thought. We also did not know how much weight the judges gave to the written pleadings as compared with the oral pleadings.

CHAPTER 7

INTERNATIONAL COUNSEL AND CONSULTANTS

Singapore is a small and relatively young country. Our legal talent pool is quite modest. We have no one yet who has distinguished himself or herself in the scholarship or practice of international law at the global level. There is no Singapore international lawyer who specialises in the field of international law litigation. In this respect, Singapore is not alone. The practice of international law is a western monopoly, with law firms in London, New York and Paris, specialising in this branch of law. Advocacy or oral pleading before the ICJ is also dominated by lawyers from Europe and America. We therefore support the Society of International Law of Singapore, the recently established Centre for International Law at the National University of Singapore Law Faculty, the Asian Society of International Law and other initiatives to nurture the growth of a new generation of Asian international lawyers. We hope that, before too long, we will see distinguished Asian international lawyers arguing cases before the International Court of Justice and other international legal forums. We would like to develop Singapore as an Asian hub for international law.

First Case in the ICJ

Pedra Branca is the first case involving Singapore in the International Court of Justice. It is the second case for Malaysia. Malaysia's first case was against Indonesia, a dispute over the sovereignty of two islands, Pulau Ligitan and Pulau Sipadan. Malaysia won the case in 2002. Three of the international Counsel who represented Malaysia in the Sipadan case also represented them in the Pedra Branca case. They were Sir Elihu Lauterpacht, Professor James Crawford and Professor Nicholas Schrijver. Three of Singapore's international Counsel, Professor Alain Pellet, Rodman Bundy and Loretta Malintoppi had represented Indonesia in the Sipadan case. This created an uncomfortable dilemma for the Malaysian team because they had to argue against the successful arguments they had put forward in the Sipadan case. Malaysia had won the Sipadan case, not based upon historic title, but on the basis of its superior record of *effectivites* or sovereign activities on the two disputed islands.

Land Reclamation Case at ITLOS

Singapore had a previous case in a different international court, the International Tribunal for the Law of the Sea (ITLOS), based in Hamburg, Germany. In 2003, Malaysia had applied to that Tribunal, requesting a provisional order to stop Singapore's land reclamation activities in the Straits of Johor, pending the outcome of arbitral proceedings which Malaysia had instituted against Singapore. Malaysia was not successful in its application. In that case, we retained two very eminent professors of international law, Professor Michael Reisman of Yale University and Professor Vaughan Lowe of Oxford University, to augment our own legal team of Chan Sek Keong, Tommy Koh, Sivakant Tiwari, Pang Khang Chau and Tan Ken Hwee.

Reasons for International Counsel

Why is it necessary for Singapore to retain international Counsel? We think there are three reasons. First, although our own international lawyers are good and competent, they lack specialised knowledge in certain areas of international law and their knowledge is textbook knowledge. Second, we need international Counsel because there are no Singaporean lawyers who have argued cases before the ICJ or ITLOS. We therefore need international Counsel who have argued cases before those courts in order to learn from their experiences and insights.

The issue of hiring international Counsel was, in fact, raised in the Singapore Parliament by a Nominated Member of Parliament, Dr Thio Li-Ann.[37] Replying to her question, Jayakumar said: "Nearly every country in the world, as far as I know, which has a case before the ICJ or other international tribunal, hires international Counsel, not because of any aspersions on their local lawyers, but for the simple reason that these international Counsel have appeared before these tribunals regularly and have pleaded before these courts. And, therefore, it is important to use their services. Let me say that, for example, in the Pedra Branca case, much of the legal work, i.e., the getting up and drafting was, in fact, done by the Singapore team."[38]

Need for Francophone International Counsel

Third, the ICJ is a bilingual forum, using English and French as the two official languages. The first language of several of the judges is French. For this reason, each country's team of advocates often includes lawyers who can speak in both languages. Another reason we should mention is that the ICJ has a large majority of judges from the civil law jurisdictions and any legal team without a civil lawyer could be at a disadvantage. The unanimous advice of our international legal advisers was to appoint one Francophone international Counsel to our team.

---

[37] DPM Professor Jayakumar (in his capacity as Minister for Law) replying to Nominated Member of Parliament Thio Li Ann during Parliament Sitting on 27 February 2008 over Budget Debate for Singapore Ministry of Law.
[38] Parliamentary Debates Singapore, Vol. 84 (27 February 2008).

We then proceeded to ask our trusted advisers to recommend the best Francophone lawyer. Professor Alain Pellet was the popular choice.

Process of Selection

How did Singapore choose its team of four international Counsel? The process began with research by AGC. AGC scanned the literature and compiled a shortlist of the world's most eminent international lawyers and those who have frequently argued cases in the ICJ. We requested a former ICJ judge to give us his shortlist of the best counsel who had appeared before him in the Court. We also consulted a trusted legal adviser in London who, for personal reasons, was unable to represent us. The final decisions were made by AGC, in consultation with Jayakumar, who kept the other key ministers informed.

Our Four International Counsel

Our final choices of international Counsel were: Ian Brownlie QC, from England, Professor Alain Pellet from France, Rodman Bundy from the United States and Loretta Malintoppi from Italy. Brownlie is sometimes referred to as the "doyen" of international lawyers. He has a formidable reputation both as a scholar and a litigator. Pellet is not only a good legal scholar but has an impeccable reputation as a litigator and is also credited with having both a brilliant and strategic mind. Bundy, an American based in Paris, was highly recommended to us as an excellent international lawyer and a brilliant advocate. Malintoppi was recommended to us as an authority on cartography but also as an excellent international lawyer.

Ian Brownlie

Ian Brownlie QC was born in Liverpool on 19 September 1932, making him the oldest member of the Singapore team, but younger

International Counsel in the Great Hall of Justice,
Peace Palace for the oral pleadings (From left: Ian Brownlie,
Alain Pellet, Rodman Bundy, Loretta Malintoppi)
(Source: Ministry of Foreign Affairs, Singapore)

than Sir Elihu Lauterpacht, counsel for Malaysia. Brownlie studied
law at Hertford College, Oxford, and King's College, Cambridge.
He was called to the Bar (Gray's Inn) in 1958. He began his
academic career in Nottingham University (1957 to 1963). He
was appointed a fellow of Wadham College, Oxford (1963 to
1976). He then became Professor of International Law at London
University (1976 to 1980). Oxford University appointed him as
the Chicele Professor of Public International Law in 1980, a
post from which he retired in 1999. He is a member and former
Chairman of the International Law Commission.

Brownlie is a prolific writer and is the author of many
publications, some of which are standard textbooks.[39]

---

[39] International Law and the Use of Force by States (1963); Principles of
International Law (1966); Encyclopaedia of African Boundaries (1979); State

Brownlie was made a Queen's Counsel in 1979 and a Bencher of Gray's Inn in 1988. He has a busy practice in international law and has appeared in 22 cases before the ICJ, representing countries from all parts of the world.

Alain Pellet

Professor Alain Pellet was born in Paris on 2 January 1947. He obtained his doctorate in public law from the University of Paris II in 1974. He began his teaching career with the University of Paris II in the same year. At the same time, he was made a professor by the University of Constantine (1974 to 1977). From 1977 to 1990, he was a professor at the University of Paris Nord. In 1980, he was also appointed as a professor at the Institute of Political Studies of Paris. Since 1990, he has been a professor at the University of Paris X (Nanterre), director of the International Law Centre of Nanterre, and director in charge of post-graduate studies in the Law of International and Community Economic Relations.

Pellet has written 11 books on law and 2 on political science. All the books are in French.

In addition to his academic career, Professor Pellet has been engaged in the practice of international law since 1993. He has been an adviser to and advocate of France and of other countries in 35 cases before the ICJ.

Pellet has served on many international organisations. Since 1990, he has been the legal adviser to the World Tourism Organisation. He has served on the UN Human Rights Commission. He is a member and former Chairman of the International

Responsibility, Part I (1983); Liber Amicorum for Lord Wilberforce (1987); The Rule of Law in International Affairs (1998); British Yearbook of International Law, Chairman of Editorial Committee (2000–present); Basic Documents in International Law (2002) (5th Edition); and Basic Documents on Human Rights (2002) (4th Edition with G.S. Goodwin-Gill).

Law Commission, and an associate member of the *Institut de Droit* International.

Rodman Bundy

Rodman Bundy is a native of Boston and comes from a very distinguished family. Two of his uncles served President John F Kennedy as National Security Adviser and Assistant Secretary for East Asia and the Pacific, respectively. Bundy did his undergraduate degree at Yale University and his law degree at Georgetown University. He first practised law in London and has been based in Paris since 1984. He speaks French fluently.

Bundy specialises in public international law, boundary disputes, oil and gas law, environmental law and international commercial arbitration. He has acted as Counsel and Advocate in 13 cases before the ICJ, including the Sipadan and Ligitan case.

Although a full-time practitioner, Bundy is also a scholar and lecturer. He is the author of many articles and teaches at the School of Oriental and African Studies, King's College of London University, and the University of Durham.

Loretta Malintoppi

Loretta Malintoppi is an Italian, the daughter of a distinguished professor of international law. She studied law at the University of Rome and at Georgetown University. After working in Rome and New York, she has been with her current law firm in Paris since 1991.

A full-time practitioner, she has also been active in legal scholarship and teaching. She is the Managing Editor of *The Law and Practice of International Courts and Tribunals*, and Editor of *International Litigation and Practice Series*. Because of her fluency in Italian, French, Spanish and English, she is a much sought after lecturer.

In the field of public international law, she has worked on a number of cases before the ICJ and in *ad hoc* arbitrations, involving, *inter alia*, maritime and land boundary disputes. She has been a Counsel and Advocate in seven cases before the ICJ, including the Sipadan and Ligitan case. We retained Malintoppi because of her expertise in cartography, but her role in the team was subsequently expanded.

History Consultants

Singapore consulted several eminent historians. We had earlier mentioned three of our own historians, Associate Professor Ernest Chew, Associate Professor Edwin Lee and Kwa Chong Guan. In addition, we consulted several foreign historians. We received valuable information, advice and insight from all of them. The one history consultant we relied the most on, with respect to the general history of the region in the 19th century, was the late Constance Mary Turnbull. We would, therefore, like to say a few words about her.

Mary Turnbull

Constance Mary Turnbull was born in England. After completing her university education, she joined the Malayan Civil Service in 1952 and was posted to Kuala Lumpur. In 1955, she made a career switch and joined the University of Malaya (located in Singapore). She taught there for 16 years before moving to Hong Kong University in 1971 where she was Professor and Head of the History Department. She retired in 1988 and returned to England. She passed away in September 2008.

Dr Turnbull was considered an expert in the histories of Singapore, Malaysia and Hong Kong. She was the author of, *inter alia*:

- *A History of Malaysia, Singapore and Brunei* (1989);

- *A History of Singapore, 1819 to 1988* (1989); and

- *The Straits Settlements, 1826 to 1867: Indian Presidency to Crown Colony* (1972).

Singapore team brainstorming in The Hague during the oral pleadings (Source: Ministry of Foreign Affairs, Singapore)

Team Building and Bonding

Having assembled a team, consisting of our own lawyers and the four international Counsel, we had to learn to work with one another, to gain each other's respect and to develop an *esprit de corps*. This happened gradually and over time as we had to begin as acquaintances and then become colleagues in a common cause and ultimately to become friends. It was fortunate that we liked and respected each other and got on well. Even when we disagreed, it never became personal. There were often disagreements, for example, between Brownlie and Pellet, but they were always about the law and about strategy and never about personal matters. Very often, Bundy would intervene and reconcile their opposing positions with an elegant compromise. Sometimes, when attempts at reaching consensus had been exhausted and the goal was still elusive, Chan Sek Keong would sum up the different positions in his usual fair, balanced and low-key manner and suggest a compromise formulation, which everyone accepted.

Observations of our International Counsel on Working with the Singapore Team

It was fortunate that an excellent working relationship was established over the years between our international Counsel and the Singapore team members. After the case was concluded, each of them gave us their observations on the case and working with us.

Ian Brownlie's observations

Brownlie made these observations:

> The oral hearings were the culmination of a procedure of dispute settlement which had been lengthy and complex. Apart from the issues of principle involved, the dispute concerned the interests of two States in the relation of geographical (and political) neighbours. These issues were of particular sensitivity for an island State.
>
> In this framework, the oral hearings were of great importance and called for intense effort, not least because the decision of the Court is, for all practical purposes, not subject to appeal. Both sides were represented by experienced teams of advocates.

In this setting the Singapore team displayed an expertise in legal knowledge and advocacy well up to international standards. The particular strengths noted by this Counsel included a very strong logistical base, which produced high grade research, a constant readiness to reassess tactics and, above all, unremitting hard work. The resilience of the team was especially evident in the provision (under pressure of time) of effective responses to the questions of Judge Keith.

Rodman Bundy's observations

Bundy highlighted the team spirit in his observations. He said:

It will be clear from the above that the presentation of a case before the ICJ entails a team effort. Every one shares a common aim. Nonetheless, it is a fact of life that these kinds of judicial proceedings can be very stressful, particularly when deadlines for written pleadings loom or oral arguments are being crafted under tight time pressure. In the Pedra Branca case, the team acted as a team, pulled together, and enjoyed working together. Even when tensions were high, team members retained their sense of humour and perspective. To me, the ability of an individual team member to take the case seriously while not taking himself or herself too seriously is an important ingredient of a successful team. Singapore should be proud of the fact that this 'esprit de corps' permeates the team it put together for the case.

Alain Pellet's observations

Pellet confided that he was "half enthusiastic" when he was first approached because quite often Singapore is viewed in France as a "soft dictatorship" at worst and at best a "heavy bureaucratic but efficient system". As an individual who did not like to be subject to many rules, he was unsure if he would be comfortable. He soon realised that "my initial perception of the Singapore social system was probably erroneous". He added that:

The Singapore team happened to generate the most pleasant and friendly atmosphere you can expect in such circumstances. Discussions were entirely free, open-minded and straightforward. All matters were taken seriously and discussions were led in depth without acrimony nor complacence until we could get a consensus or, in the worst cases, a fully enlightened majority decision.

In case an apparent disagreement arose, discussions were held as long as necessary in order to find the best solution and further researches were made by our Singapore colleagues as often and as long as deemed useful. This was true as well when we were preparing the written pleadings as during the hearings where we have benefited of all the needed assistance — and much more.

Among more than 35 cases before the ICJ and representing 20 States or so, my involvement in the Pedra Branca case has been one of the most enjoyable, probably the most satisfactory, experience of that kind I ever had in a case before the World Court (or indeed, before any international court or tribunal).

Loretta Malintoppi's observations

When States decide to litigate their legal differences it is in my view extremely important that the relevant officials of the States concerned play a major role. No foreign counsel, no matter how well-known and knowledgeable in the field of international law, can replace the team of lawyers and experts of the State concerned. In the case of Singapore, the in-house team had such an extensive knowledge of the case that it provided invaluable assistance to counsel. For my part, I wound up learning a great deal from the members of the Singapore team. Without the Singapore team, my work would have been much more difficult, and thanks to their support and encouragement, I worked with renewed confidence and enthusiasm.

Singapore's team of advocates (From left: Alain Pellet,
Rodman Bundy, Ian Brownlie, Jayakumar, Chan Sek Keong,
Chao Hick Tin, Tommy Koh and Loretta Malintoppi)
(Source: Tan Ken Hwee)

The atmosphere of camaraderie and *esprit de corps* that
characterised the Singapore team both during the written
and oral proceedings was exceptional. I have been working
with a number of governmental teams in State-to-State
disputes, but the Singapore team will always stand out as
one of the most competent, efficient and good-humoured
in-house teams I have had the good fortune to work with.

CHAPTER 8

PREPARING FOR THE ORAL PLEADINGS

Conversation with Malaysian Agent

The Singapore Agent Tommy Koh called the Malaysian Agent, Tan Sri Abdul Kadir Mohamad, an old friend from their Washington days, on the telephone on 3 January 2006. He had called for two reasons: to confirm that the two sides would not seek a fourth round of written pleadings and to agree to request the Court to grant us an early date for the oral hearings. The next step was for the two Co-Agents to write a joint letter to the Registrar, informing him that we would not request for a Rejoinder and proposing the number of sessions for the oral proceedings.

Procedural Meeting with ICJ and Malaysia

Article 31 of the Rules of Court states that, "… the President shall ascertain the views of the Parties with regard to questions of procedure. For this purpose he shall summon the agents of the parties to meet him as soon as possible after their appointment …."

The President of the ICJ recused herself from sitting in the case. Accordingly, the Vice-President, Awn Shawkat Al-Khasawneh,

Malaysian Foreign Minister Rais Yatim, Tan Sri Abdul Kadir
Mohamad and Ambassador Noor Farida Ariffin meeting
Tommy Koh at the Court (Source: Ministry of
Foreign Affairs, Singapore)

became the Acting President.[40] Incidentally, the President had to
recuse herself because she had earlier given advice to Singapore
on the dispute. The Acting President and the Registrar met with
representatives of Malaysia and Singapore at the Peace Palace
on 12 April 2006. Malaysia was represented by its Co-Agent,
Ambassador Noor Farida Ariffin, and its international Counsel,
Sir Elihu Lauterpacht and Professor Nicholas Schrijver. Singapore
was represented by its Agent, Co-Agent, international Counsel
Professor Alain Pellet, and government officials Foo Chi Hsia
and Tan Ken Hwee.

At the meeting, the Court informed the two parties that the
oral hearings would take place from 6 to 23 November 2007.
It was agreed that each party would have four half-days to

---

[40] See Chapter 9.

present its case and two half-days to reply to the other. Party "X" would present its case on the mornings of 6, 7, 8 and 9 November. Party "Y" would present its case on the mornings of 13, 14, 15 and 16 November. Party "X" would reply on the mornings of 19 and 20 November. Party "Y" would reply on the afternoons of 22 and 23 November. It may be noted that the ICJ is very punctilious in ensuring that states appearing before it are given an equal amount of time to prepare and present their opening and closing speeches.

Who Would Go First?

The question arose as to who would plead first and who would follow. Singapore suggested that the Court should follow the normal practice of proceeding in alphabetical order of the names in English of the two countries. Following this practice, Malaysia would go first. Sir Elihu Lauterpacht disagreed, presumably because he wanted Malaysia to go second and to have the last word. He suggested tossing a coin. Singapore rejected his proposal as being too flippant. Since the two sides could not agree on another way to break the impasse, they agreed to leave it to the Court to decide.

On 22 September 2006, the Registrar informed the two parties that the Court had drawn lots and the result was that Singapore would go first. This was a disappointment as initially Singapore was of the view that if Malaysia were to start first, it would be much easier for Singapore to rebut Malaysia's arguments and also have the last word. Nevertheless, Singapore took the setback in its stride and proceeded on the basis that in starting first we would be able to make a strong and lasting impression on the judges while their minds were fresh. As it turned out, Malaysia was not able to make much of the advantage of going second, except to introduce a new argument during the second round, knowing full well that Singapore would have no opportunity to rebut the argument.

The team brainstorming at our embassy in London in June 2007
(Source: Ministry of Foreign Affairs, Singapore)

Meetings with International Counsel

The Singapore team and its international Counsel met twice
to prepare for the oral hearings. The first meeting was held
on 28 and 29 September 2006 in Singapore and the second
meeting was held on 11 and 12 June 2007 in London. These
preparatory meetings were very intensive. All the draft speeches
were rigorously reviewed paragraph by paragraph and changes
were proposed to both the form and substance of the arguments.
Equally important, we were able to agree on the issues of
law and fact to be allocated to the four Singapore advocates,
Tommy Koh (the Agent), Jayakumar, Chan Sek Keong and Chao
Hick Tin, and the four international Counsel, Brownlie, Pellet,
Bundy and Malintoppi, the order in which they would speak,
the amount of time allocated to each speaker, and the graphics
to be used by each of them.

Singapore team reviewing preparations after one of the
rehearsals at MFA Headquarters in October 2007
(Source: Ministry of Foreign Affairs, Singapore)

Rehearsals in Singapore — Even Before Supreme Court Judges!

The four Singapore advocates decided to hold a rehearsal, which, was held at MFA on 11 October 2007. The four speakers were filmed and their speeches timed in the presence of other members of the team and MFA officers. After the rehearsal, there was a discussion on both the content and delivery of the speeches. It was agreed that changes should be made to the speeches to make them tighter and that a second rehearsal be held at MFA on 25 October. At Chan Sek Keong's suggestion, both he and Jayakumar even had yet a third rehearsal in the Supreme Court. They "pleaded" before two Judges of Appeal, V K Rajah and Andrew Phang, to test their reaction to the logic and substance of the arguments. The Singapore Judges' reaction was positive.

Late night sessions at the Crowne Plaza Promenade Hotel in
The Hague to put finishing touches to arguments in oral pleadings
(Source: Ministry of Foreign Affairs, Singapore)

Mood and Assessment

The mood of the Singapore team before its departure for The Hague was calm, confident and upbeat. Members of the Singapore team felt that they had a superior case to that put forward by Malaysia. They were confident that their arguments that Pedra Branca was *terra nullius* in 1847, that the British had taken lawful possession of the island between 1847 and 1851 as a sovereign and had acted as such ever since, and the long and continuous *effectivites*, formed a very strong foundation for Singapore's case. The Singapore team hoped that their arguments on these three points would prevail over any attempt by Malaysia to try to exploit the ambiguity in the Temenggong's reply to Governor Butterworth's request of 1844 to erect a lighthouse on an island adjacent to mainland Johor, and other weaknesses in Singapore's case. For example, the failure of Singapore to make an express declaration that Pedra Branca was Singapore's territory, or by unambiguously referring to it as such in any legislation, or by depicting it as such in any of its maps or other official records. Although confident, we reminded ourselves not to be smug nor underestimate the strength of the Malaysian legal team which included several international legal luminaries. We knew they were going to give us a good fight.

Fire in our Hotel

Members of the Singapore team arrived at The Hague from 28 October to 2 November 2007. The advance team, consisting of officers from our Embassy in Brussels, IT and communications support staff, and MFA and AGC officers arrived from 28 to 30 October 2007. The team had also conducted multiple reconnaissance trips to The Hague prior to the oral hearings to ensure that all the logistical details were in order or taken care of. They set up a fully equipped secretariat at the Crowne Plaza Promenade Hotel. This involved a tremendous amount of work that included the installation of computers, office

Pang Khang Chau checking to ensure that all documents
were safe in his laptop computer after the evacuation due to
a fire in Crowne Plaza Promenade Hotel
(Source: Ministry of Foreign Affairs, Singapore)

equipment, a library, pantry, and the provision of all necessary
office accessories. Disaster almost struck on the night of 30
October at about 11.00 pm, when a fire broke out in our hotel.
The fire had started in the hotel's kitchen. The fire alarm went
off and soon, several fire engines arrived at the hotel. Some of
our colleagues were working in their rooms whilst Senior State
Counsel Pang Khang Chau and Brussels Mission First Secretary
Yvonne Elizabeth Chee were still working in the Secretariat. When
the smoke from the fire became a hazard, the hotel requested
everyone to evacuate the building. Khang Chau and Yvonne
were able to contact their colleagues. Those in their rooms called
the hotel reception to check on the situation upon hearing the
fire alarms in their rooms. In their hurry, some had left their
passports in their rooms. However, all of them remembered
to take their laptops with them! Soon order was restored and

they went back to work. As part of the preparatory work, members of the Singapore team also visited the Peace Palace on 1 and 2 November to see the Court room, test its acoustics and IT system, visit the library, the room allocated to Singapore for the use of its team, and the press centre. Mrs Laurence Blairon, the Head of Press and Information of the Registry, welcomed us warmly and gave us a conducted tour of the Peace Palace.

Agent's Illness

On 3, 4 and 5 November (Saturday, Sunday and Monday), the whole team assembled at the meeting room in our Secretariat to go over the texts of the various speeches. The meetings were chaired by Chan Sek Keong. The procedure used for the preparation of the written pleadings was followed and we went through the texts, paragraph by paragraph. The job was done by Monday. The only untoward development was that Tommy Koh, our Agent, contracted a severe cough and cold that caused him almost to lose his voice. This was not a good beginning since the Agent was the first speaker for Singapore, and would be speaking two days later. Jayakumar insisted that Tommy see a doctor, which he did on Monday, 5 November, receiving medication to relieve his severe ailment. This was reinforced by manuka honey from Foo Chi Hsia and Chinese herbal medicine from Philip Ong! The team went to bed on Monday night ready to do battle the next day.

Sleepless at The Hague

However, not all the members of the Singapore team were able to go to bed early. AGC, Supreme Court and MFA staff, including our Co-Agent, Ambassador in Brussels Anil Kumar Nayar,[41]

---

[41] After the previous Co-Agent Walter Woon completed his posting to the Netherlands, Anil Kumar Nayar assumed post and assumed appointment as Co-Agent on 14 March 2007.

Anil Kumar Nayar, Parry Oei and Sivakant Tiwari with the
Singapore team helping to prepare the Judges' folders
for the oral pleadings into the wee hours of the night
(Source: Ministry of Foreign Affairs, Singapore)

our Chief Hydrographer Parry Oei and Tiwari, stayed up until
the early hours of the night preparing 80 Judges' Folders and
checking for accuracy. It was all hands on deck! It has become
the practice for the parties appearing before the ICJ to prepare
folders for the judges in order to help them follow the oral
hearings. The folders contain the texts of the speeches by
the advocates to be delivered that day. In addition, they also
include copies of the documents, graphics and powerpoint slides.
However, only documents which are contained in the party's
written pleadings and their Annexes may be cited. The team
preparing the Judges' Folders had to stay up very late every
night because some colleagues continued polishing the texts of
their statements until late at night. Once all the documents had
been compiled, the team had to photocopy them and file them
in the folders to be ready to be delivered to the Registry early
the next morning.

Birthday celebrations at The Hague during the oral pleadings
Top left: Tommy Koh's birthday (Source: Ministry of
Foreign Affairs, Singapore)
Top right: Chan Sek Keong's birthday (Source: Tan Ken Hwee)
Bottom: Yvonne Elizabeth Chee's birthday
(Source: Ministry of Foreign Affairs, Singapore)

CHAPTER 9

THE ORAL PROCEEDINGS

T he oral proceedings were held in the Great Hall of Justice of the Peace Palace, which is the seat of the ICJ. It is an impressive building, with a clock tower on the left and a smaller tower on the right. The building is approached through a pair of iron gates, a large garden and an elegant drive-way. The Peace Palace was built in 1913, with a generous grant by the American philanthropist, Andrew Carnegie, as the home of the Permanent Court of Arbitration. In 1919, the

The Peace Palace, The Hague, Netherlands
(Source: Ministry of Foreign Affairs, Singapore)

Inside the Peace Palace
(Source: Ministry of Foreign Affairs, Singapore)

League of Nations accepted the offer of the Dutch Government to make the Peace Palace the seat of the Permanent Court of International Justice (PCIJ), which began to function in 1922. It ceased operations upon the outbreak of the Second World War, and was dissolved in 1945 to make way for the ICJ, which was established by the UN Charter. Since 1946, the Peace Palace has been the seat of the ICJ.

The ICJ Judges

The ICJ has 15 judges. They are elected simultaneously by the UN General Assembly and the Security Council. A judge must obtain a simple majority in both bodies to be elected. If there is more than one candidate for a vacancy, the candidate with

Singapore and Malaysia's Agents with the ICJ Acting President
(From left: Tan Sri Abdul Kadir Mohamad, Awn Shawkat Al-Khasawneh
and Tommy Koh) (Source: Ministry of Foreign Affairs, Singapore)

the highest number of votes wins. A judge serves a term of nine
years, subject to the possibility of seeking re-election. The 15
seats on the Court are allocated among the regional groups of
the UN as follows: Africa 3, Latin America and the Caribbean
2, Asia 3, Western Europe and others 5, and Eastern Europe 2.
This gives the West 7 out of 15 seats on the Court. Once every
three years, the judges elect, by secret ballot, their President and
Vice-President. The current President is Dame Rosalyn Higgins
of the United Kingdom and the Vice-President is Awn Shawkat
Al-Khasawneh of Jordan.

President Higgins Recuses Herself

Rosalyn Higgins had a brilliant academic career that led to an
appointment as Professor of International Law at the London
School of Economics. In 1994, Singapore sought her legal advice

on Singapore's claim to Pedra Branca. She gave a positive opinion. It was for this reason that she had to recuse herself from the case when it came before the ICJ. The Vice-President, Al-Khasawneh, automatically presided over the case as Acting President.

The Judges Hosted Lunches and Receptions for Both Sides

We were pleasantly surprised when the Acting President of the Court and other Judges invited us to lunches on two occasions. They invited the Agents and leading members of both legal teams. Most of the ICJ Judges turned up at these lunches, which were held in a Thai-Chinese restaurant. They also hosted a separate event just for the international Counsel of both countries. In addition, they hosted a cocktail reception for all the members of the delegations of both countries.

These were good gestures on their part. Naturally, at all these functions, both the Judges as well as members of the two sides were careful not to discuss this case, which was before the Court. We found it interesting that the Judges commented that both teams from Malaysia and Singapore seemed to display a civilised and courteous approach towards each other. They said this made it easier for the Judges to host such functions.

Judges *Ad Hoc*

Under Article 31, paragraphs 1 and 2 of the Statute of the ICJ, a party not having a judge of its nationality on the bench may choose a person to sit as judge *ad hoc* in that specific case. Neither Singapore nor Malaysia had a national on the ICJ bench and both chose to appoint a judge *ad hoc*. Malaysia appointed Professor Christopher Dugard of South Africa. Singapore appointed Dr P S Rao of India. A judge *ad hoc* has to make the same solemn declaration as an elected judge to act "on the basis of the law, independently of all outside influence or interventions whatsoever". He takes part in any decision concerning the case on terms of complete equality with his elected colleagues. What is the rationale for having a judge *ad hoc*? It is thought that it is useful for the Court to have participating in its deliberations two persons more familiar with the views of each of the parties than the elected judges may be. Does the inclusion of judges *ad hoc* make any difference to the outcomes of the Court's decisions? It would appear from the ICJ's own study (The International Court of Justice, 2004, 5th Edition, at page 31) that it does not. With the addition of Judge Dugard and Judge Rao, the Court hearing the Pedra Branca case had 16 judges. If there had been a tie in this case, the presiding judge would have a casting vote.

The Great Hall of Justice

The Great Hall of Justice is a bright and cheerful room, with large stained glass windows that let in a lot of natural light. The room has extensive wood panels which are of a reddish warm hue. The floor is covered by a large carpet of cheerful colours. The judges sit at a long table with curved ends on both sides and covered by green baize. The judges filed in from the left with Judge Dugard sitting at the extreme right and Judge Rao at the extreme left. The Acting President sat in the middle of the table and the Registrar at the extreme left, after Judge Rao. The judges' table rests on a raised platform. For the members of the Singapore team, appearing for the first time as counsel before the Court was a very moving experience.

The Opening Day

The oral proceedings began on the morning of Tuesday, 6 November 2007. When the Agent awoke that morning, his voice had become a hoarse whisper. In desperation, he phoned his doctor in Singapore, Professor Luke Tan of the National University Hospital, for advice. Professor Tan confirmed the Dutch doctor, Dr Einhorn's prescription but advised the Agent to double the dosage of the medication. By 10.15am, when the

The Court in session in the Great Hall of Justice
(Source: IFS Audiovisueel)

Acting President called on him to speak, his voice had improved. It was weak but audible. It got better as he spoke.

Singapore Greets Malaysia

The Singapore delegation arrived early at the Peace Palace and went to the Singapore party room to robe. The four Singaporeans wore their black legal gowns. Each of our international Counsel dressed according to his or her national legal attire. Brownlie was dressed like an English barrister, Pellet in a flaming red gown, Malintoppi in her Italian legal gown and Bundy in a suit. We entered the Great Hall two abreast and greeted our Malaysian colleagues who were already seated. Malaysia occupied the table on the right and Singapore on the left. The lectern was in the middle. We acted in a friendly and professional manner towards our Malaysian colleagues. The Registrar subsequently thanked us for creating a good working relationship between the two parties, which facilitated the smooth flow of the proceedings. He said that in a recent case, the two parties were barely on talking terms and this made the work of the Court very difficult.

Day 1 for Singapore

At 10.00am, the proceedings began. The Acting President introduced the two judges *ad hoc* who took their solemn declarations. He proceeded to recall the background of the case and then called upon the Agent of Singapore to begin.

Agent's Speech[42]
(IFS Audiovisueel)

The Singapore Agent (Tommy Koh) began by extending his fraternal greetings to the Malaysian Agent, whom he described as "an old friend", and described the Malaysian Co-Agent as a "much admired" Ambassador at The Hague. Next, Tommy explained to the Court the importance which Singapore attaches to the rule of law and international law and Singapore's preference to submit disputes that cannot be resolved by negotiations to arbitration or adjudication. He spoke about the close historical, economic and cultural ties that exist between Malaysia and Singapore. He also introduced the members of the Singapore delegation and explained why Deputy Prime Minister Professor S Jayakumar and Chief Justice Chan Sek Keong were members of the team.

The Agent then outlined Singapore's case as follows:

- Pedra Branca was *terra nullius* in 1847;

- The British took lawful possession of the island in 1847 and completed building Horsburgh Lighthouse in 1851;

---

[42] For verbatim records of all the speeches during the oral pleadings, please refer to: <http://www.icj-cij.org/docket/index.php?p1=3&p2=3&k=2b&case=130&code=masi&p3=2>.

- The pattern of activities and official acts undertaken by agents of the British Crown during that period, culminating in the official inauguration of the Horsburgh Lighthouse in 1851, were clear and unequivocal manifestations of the British intention to claim sovereignty over the island;

- The said activities were peaceful and public and elicited no opposition from Johor or any other power; and

- Singapore's title had been maintained by our continuous, open and effective display of State authority over Pedra Branca and its territorial waters for over 130 years until 1979, when Malaysia first advanced a claim to the island.

Finally, he drew attention to a number of facts which were inconsistent with Malaysia's claim, such as:

- A letter from Johor's Acting State Secretary informing Singapore that Johor (in 1953 when it was a sovereign State) did not claim ownership over Pedra Branca; and

- Six maps published by Malaysia's highest national mapping authority specifically attributing Pedra Branca to Singapore.

Chao Hick Tin's Speech
(IFS Audiovisueel)

The Attorney-General's speech focused on three points:

- The physical and geographical settings of Pedra Branca, Middle Rocks and South Ledge;

- An outline of certain key events relevant to the case; and

- The developments leading up to the dispute and its submission to the Court.

In their written pleadings, Malaysia's team had tried to convince the Court that Pedra Branca, Middle Rocks and South Ledge should not be treated as a single entity but as separate entities. Fearing that the Court would award sovereignty over Pedra Branca to Singapore, Malaysia wanted Middle Rocks and South Ledge as a consolation prize. Chao Hick Tin argued that Pedra Branca and Middle Rocks are part of the same rock formation, connected by a submerged bank and should be treated as an indivisible whole. South Ledge, a low tide elevation, lying within the territorial waters of Pedra Branca and Middle Rocks, belongs to whoever has sovereignty over Pedra Branca.

The highlight of Chao Hick Tin's speech was the playing of an audio recording of the May 1980 press conference in Singapore, held by the Prime Ministers of Malaysia and Singapore, during which the Prime Minister of Malaysia, Hussein Onn, was asked a question about Malaysia's claim to Pedra Branca. Prime Minister Hussein Onn said: "We are also looking into the question because this is not very clear to us with regard to the island." The playing of the audio recording had the effect of demonstrating Malaysia's uncertainty, at the highest level of government, over its claim. We noticed some knowing smiles from the bench and some embarrassed smiles from a few members of the Malaysian delegation.

Chan Sek Keong's Speech
(IFS Audiovisueel)

Chief Justice Chan Sek Keong gave a learned speech refuting Malaysia's claim that Johor had an original title to Pedra Branca. He showed, by citing all the established authorities on the subject, that in a Malay Sultanate (the Johor Sultanate included), sovereignty was based on control of people rather than control of territory. This meant that the Johor Sultanate did not have clearly defined boundaries and it was difficult to determine with accuracy the territorial extent of the Sultanate at any time. Malaysia had claimed an original title to Pedra Branca, and therefore had to produce clear evidence of such title. Malaysia had failed to do so. There was no evidence that Pedra Branca belonged to the Johor Sultanate at any point in its history and certainly not at the beginning of the 19th century. He also showed that Pedra Branca did not become part of the new Johor after 1824, when the Anglo-Dutch Treaty established an international boundary between territories under Britain and the Netherlands, and as a consequence never became part of Malaysia. As Chan Sek Keong explained to the Court, "The origins of the Anglo-Dutch Treaty can be traced back to two events — the French conquest of the Netherlands in 1795, and the death of Sultan Mahmud III of Johor in 1812, leaving a succession dispute between his two sons, Hussein and Abdul Rahman. In 1795, Britain took control of the Dutch colonial possessions in the East to deny them to the French. When war ended in 1814, Britain agreed to return these possessions to the Dutch. A number of disputes arose between the British and the Dutch regarding the British occupation of these possessions. These disputes led to the negotiations which culminated in the signing of the Anglo-Dutch Treaty." Sek Keong had clearly mastered his brief on this aspect of Malay history.

Alain Pellet's Speech

(IFS Audiovisueel)

The fourth and final speaker for the day was Professor Alain Pellet. Delivered in French with great panache, Pellet's presentation examined the documents that Malaysia had produced to support her claim of an original title. He went through each of the documents and showed that they did not support Malaysia's contention. He chastised Malaysia for mis-translating a letter from the Dutch Governor in Malacca to the Council of the Dutch East Indies Company in Batavia. Malaysia had produced a Vietnamese document of 1833 reporting the account of a Vietnamese envoy describing Pedra Branca as a port covered with forest and greenery with reed huts. Some of the judges laughed quietly when the account was projected on the screen together with pictures of Pedra Branca as a barren rock.

Reflections on Day 1

After the Court hearing, the Singapore delegation returned to have lunch together to assess our performance on the first day. The consensus reached was that we had a good and impactful first day. All our presentations, including the powerpoint graphics, audio recording and Judges' Folders went according to plan. All our speakers delivered their statements well and seemed able to carry the Court with them on our key arguments.

Day 2: 7 November 2007

Pellet continued with his presentation on Malaysia's failure to produce any documentary proof of its original title. He dealt with Malaysia's reliance on the 1824 Anglo-Dutch Treaty, the so-called 1824 map, the grant made by Sultan Abdul Rahman (based in Riau) to his brother, Sultan Hussein (based in Singapore) in his letter dated 25 June 1825, and the Treaty concluded by Crawfurd with the Sultan and Temenggong of Johor, on 2 August 1824. Pellet showed that Malaysia had failed to establish the existence of an original title for Johor over Pedra Branca. Since Pedra Branca did not come under the sovereignty of Johor, there was no question of the Sultan or Temenggong of Johor giving Butterworth permission in 1844 to build Horsburgh Lighthouse on Pedra Branca.

In the course of his speech, Pellet drew the Court's attention to the misleading manner in which Malaysia had used the written pleadings. He cited the example in which Malaysia had quoted an extract from J T Thomson's account of the Temenggong's visit to Pedra Branca. By conveniently dropping a part of the quotation, the Malaysians had tried to change the significance of the event, from one in which the Temenggong had visited the island in a sampan provided by the British Governor, to one in which he visited the island in his own boat and as the sovereign. Some of the judges sat up and took notes when this was pointed out by Pellet.

Ian Brownlie's Speech

(IFS Audiovisueel)

The rest of the morning was taken up by Brownlie's speech. He gave a detailed account of how title to Pedra Branca was acquired by the British Crown in accordance with the legal principles governing acquisition of territory in the period 1847 to 1851. In doing so, Brownlie also gave several examples of Malaysia's selective use of legal authorities. Malaysia relied on the 5th Edition of Oppenheim's International Law (published in 1937), to argue that the taking of legal possession of a territory can only be done by a settlement on the territory. Brownlie pointed out that in the more recent 9th Edition, Oppenheim explained that while earlier editions had suggested that settlement is a *sine qua non* of effective occupation, this only applies to large areas of habitable terrain and might not apply to offshore islets which could hardly be "settled" in any true sense of the word, but could nevertheless still be "occupied". Another example cited by Brownlie was the way in which Malaysia's Counter-Memorial had deliberately omitted half of a sentence from paragraph 17 of the UK's application to the ICJ in the Antarctica case.

The examples given by Pellet and Brownlie suggested a certain sense of desperation on the part of the Malaysian team. Mis-translating a text, suppressing parts of quotations, the selective use of legal authorities, are tactics that would not be tolerated in any domestic court of law. We were both puzzled and disappointed that they resorted to such tactics before the highest Court in the world.

Day 3: 8 November 2007

On the third day, three of our international Counsel, Bundy, Malintoppi and Pellet addressed the Court.

Rodman Bundy's Speech
(IFS Audiovisueel)

Bundy did a brilliant job in presenting the wide range of sovereign activities undertaken by Singapore after 1851, after title had been acquired. The *effectivites* include issuing notices to mariners, flying the Singapore marine ensign, enacting legislation, maintaining and constructing lighthouse-related and non lighthouse-related facilities, controlling visits and access to the island, collecting meteorological data, conducting naval patrols and investigating shipwrecks. This continuous exercise of state authority, completely unopposed by Malaysia, confirmed and maintained Singapore's title over Pedra Branca.

Bundy had represented Indonesia and Sir Elihu Lauterpacht had represented Malaysia in the Sipadan and Ligitan case. Bundy cleverly used Malaysia's own arguments in that case against them. He projected a quotation from the speech of Sir Elihu on the screen. By changing the word "Malaysia" to "Singapore" and "Indonesia" to "Malaysia", he showed that Singapore's argument in the Pedra Branca case was similar to Malaysia's argument in the Sipadan case. Malaysia, meanwhile, had done a U-turn and was refuting her own arguments in the Sipadan case. Bundy's demonstration of Malaysia's doctrinal inconsistency must have caused some embarrassment to the Malaysians.

Loretta Malintoppi's Speech
(IFS Audiovisueel)

Malintoppi addressed the reverse side of the coin, that is, Malaysia's absence of *effectivites*. She said that Malaysia could not point to a single act of administration and control over Pedra Branca. She systematically showed that the acts referred to by Malaysia, in its written pleadings, were episodic and did not qualify as sovereign activities. If the case were to be decided on the basis of the two party's competing *effectivites*, it would be a one-sided contest as Malaysia had no *effectivites* to speak of.

Alain Pellet

Pellet then addressed the Court on Malaysia's recognition of Singapore's sovereignty over Pedra Branca. These included giving permission to a Malaysian naval officer in 1974 to conduct a survey and other activities around Pedra Branca, as well as a request by the Malaysian High Commission in 1980 for permission to lay an underwater cable in the waters near Pedra Branca. He also pointed to the absence of protest by Malaysia to Singapore's activities on the island and its surrounding waters. As for the Malaysian argument that there was no need to protest because Singapore's activities did not necessitate a protest, Pellet pointed out that Malaysia had been protesting against the same and similar activities subsequent to the crystallisation of the dispute.

Day 4: 9 November 2007

This was the final day for Singapore's presentations in round one. The morning began with Bundy, who completed his presentation on the Straits Lights System. He was followed by Malintoppi, who spoke on the significance of maps and third state recognition. Pellet then spoke on Middle Rocks and South Ledge. Finally, Jayakumar made a concluding statement.

Straits Lights System

Bundy gave a lucid presentation on the Straits Lights System. He pointed out that there was a difference between Pedra Branca and lighthouses built on islands or territories over which Singapore had no sovereignty, viz., Pulau Pisang, Cape Rachado and Pulau Aur. He argued that Malaysia recognised that it had no sovereignty over Pedra Branca because whilst it had instructed Singapore to lower its marine ensign flying over Pulau Pisang, it did not make a similar demand in the case of Pedra Branca.

Maps and Third State Recognition

Malintoppi drew the Court's attention to the series of six Malaysian maps, the latest of which was published in 1975, attributing Pedra Branca to Singapore. She reviewed all the maps which Malaysia had adduced to support her claim of an immemorial title. She dismissed the significance of Malaysia's cartographic evidence. She also listed the examples of third state recognition of Singapore's sovereignty over Pedra Branca.

Middle Rocks and South Ledge

Pellet elaborated on Chao Hick Tin's arguments that Pedra Branca, Middle Rocks and South Ledge should be treated as a group.

Jayakumar's Concluding Statement

(IFS Audiovisueel)

Jayakumar made a concluding statement, pulling together all the arguments in the preceding 12 statements as put forward by Singapore over the past four days. Our key arguments were briefly restated. We hoped the statement would have an impact and leave the judges with the clear impression that Singapore had sovereignty over Pedra Branca for 130 years before Malaysia suddenly sprang a surprise by publishing a map in 1979 claiming that Pedra Branca belonged to Malaysia. We also hoped the fact that our concluding statement made by our Deputy Prime Minister would have conveyed to the Court the importance and seriousness that Singapore attached to the case.

CHAPTER 10

MALAYSIA'S FIRST ROUND

Malaysia's first round took place on the mornings of 13, 14, 15 and 16 November. Who were the members of the Malaysian team? The Malaysian Agent was Tan Sri Abdul Kadir Mohamad, who was also Malaysia's Agent in the Sipadan and Ligitan case. The Co-Agent was Ambassador Noor Farida Ariffin, Malaysia's Ambassador to the Netherlands. The other members of the Malaysian delegation included:

- Dato Seri Syed Hamid Albar, Foreign Minister;

- Tan Sri Abdul Gani Patel, Attorney-General;

- Sir Elihu Lauterpacht QC, Honorary Professor of International Law, Cambridge University;

- Professor James Crawford, Whewell Professor of International Law, Cambridge University;

- Professor Nicholas Schrijver, Professor of Public International Law, Leiden University;

- Professor Marcelo Kohen, Professor of Public International Law, Graduate Institute of International Studies, Geneva; and

- Dr Penelope Newell, Lecturer, Downing College, Cambridge University.

The entire Malaysian delegation consisted of about 60 members, about double the size of Singapore's delegation.

Three Objectives of Malaysia's Case

Malaysia's strategy was based on multiple prongs. The first was to rely on the geographical fact of Pedra Branca as part of the Malay cultural and political landscape by describing it as part of the Malay world in order to assert that the island had always been a territorial possession of the Johor-Riau-Lingga Sultanate. Malaysia argued that when the Sultanate was divided into two spheres of influence by the Anglo-Dutch Treaty of 1824, Pedra Branca fell within the British and northern part of the Sultanate. Malaysia alleged that it was the successor through the State of Johor. This argument that Malaysia had an original or historical title to Pedra Branca, if accepted, would form the basis of this alleged historical or original title. Malaysia would go on to assert that Singapore, in spite of having been in undisturbed possession of Pedra Branca for more than 150 years, could not have acquired title to the island because international law did not and does not recognise the doctrine of prescription. The essence of prescription is the usurpation of the territory of another sovereign which, over time, becomes valid because of the latter's consent or acquiescence.

The second prong was that, in any event, the Sultanate gave permission to the British to build Horsburgh Lighthouse on Pedra Branca as the Temenggong's reply of 1845 to Governor Butterworth's missing 1844 letter had referred to "any spot deemed eligible" which would apply to Pedra Branca. In Malaysia's contention, the case could be decided on a single issue in her favour, that is, that Pedra Branca had always been part of the Sultanate and therefore could not have been *terra nullius* in 1844, as asserted by Singapore.

Malaysia had another subsidiary argument to deny Singapore's acquisition of title to Pedra Branca by taking possession of it in 1847 and thereafter carrying out state activities on it for more than 150 years. The argument was that Singapore was merely using the island for the purpose of administering a lighthouse and nothing more. The argument was that Singapore had never asserted or claimed sovereignty over the island, but was merely a lighthouse keeper.

The last prong in Malaysia's strategy was that if the ICJ awarded sovereignty over Pedra Branca to Singapore, it should award sovereignty over Middle Rocks and South Ledge to Malaysia as Singapore had never exercised sovereign rights over the two maritime features. Finally, in a bid to influence the ICJ, Malaysia expressly informed the ICJ that it would allow Singapore to continue to operate the lighthouse if the ICJ held that Pedra Branca belonged to Malaysia.

Mysterious Photograph of Pedra Branca

During her presentation, the Malaysian Co-Agent Ambassador Noor Farida Ariffin sprang a surprise by showing the Court a photograph of Pedra Branca, which we had never seen before. Malaysia had not included this photograph in any of their written pleadings.[43] This photograph turned out to be a public relations disaster for Malaysia because it had been distorted to support Malaysia's point that Pedra Branca was near to the coast of Johor. The photograph was ostensibly downloaded from a blog website, <www.leuchttrum3.blogspot.com>. This blog site was most unusual as it had been created only a month before the date fixed for the oral hearing before the Court.[44] Moreover, the photograph in question was posted on the website on 2 November 2007, four days before the commencement of the oral hearings. It remains unclear who the author of the

---

[43] ICJ's rules do not allow the introduction of new documents after the close of the written pleadings (except with the permission of the Court or the consent of the other side) unless the document "is part of a publication readily available". (Reference: Art 56 of the Rules of Court, especially para. 4 of Art 56.)

[44] The first post was on 24 October 2007.

**Mysterious photograph of Pedra Branca and Horsburgh Lighthouse
with the Johor Mainland in the background**
(Source: Judges' Folder, Oral Pleadings of Malaysia, Case
concerning Sovereignty over Pedra Branca/Pulau Batu Puteh, Middle
Rocks and South Ledge (Malaysia/Singapore), Volume 2, Tab 78).

**Photograph of Pedra Branca and Horsburgh Lighthouse with the
Johor Mainland in the background taken by MPA**
(Source: Judges' Folder, Oral Pleadings of Singapore, Case
concerning Sovereignty over Pedra Branca/Pulau Batu Puteh, Middle
Rocks and South Ledge (Malaysia/Singapore), Volume 2, Tab 6).

blog was. The blog site also stopped being updated soon after the oral pleadings were concluded, with the last post on 30 November 2007.

When the Singapore delegation saw this photograph projected on the screen in the Court, we knew at once that there was something wrong with the photograph. Many of us who had been to the area knew that the Johor coast was shown as being much too near Pedra Branca and the hill, Bukit Pelali or Mount Berbukit appeared much too high. In fact, it appeared to loom over Pedra Branca. After Malaysia had completed her pleadings for the day and the Court adjourned, our hydrographer, Parry Oei, who was in our team, emailed and telephoned his colleagues at MPA to take photographs at the actual location and from approximately the same geographical co-ordinates. This would enable us to challenge the authenticity of Malaysia's photograph. The next morning, MPA officials went to Pedra Branca and took more than a hundred photographs of Pedra Branca and emailed the most suitable of these pictures for us to show to the Court in our reply.

On 20 November, when Chao Hick Tin replied in the second round, he was able to demonstrate to the Court, by comparing the Malaysian photo taken from a website with a real photograph taken at the same location by MPA, that Malaysia's photograph had been taken with a telephoto lens which increased the height of the hill in the background by a factor of seven to give the impression that Pedra Branca was nearer to the Johor coast than it really was.

We believed that Chao's demonstration made an impact on the judges. We noticed one judge passing a note to one of his colleagues. We also noticed that a member of the Malaysian delegation was clearly so embarrassed by the *faux pas* that she spontaneously covered her face with both hands.

Strengths and Weaknesses after First Round

Our assessment of the Malaysian team's performance at the end of their first round was that they had been very eloquent and inventive. They had glossed over Singapore's strong points and focused their attacks on our weak points. They had reiterated their basic point that Johor had an original title to Pedra Branca inherited from the Sultanate, and that Horsburgh Lighthouse had been constructed by the British with Johor's consent. They attacked our argument that the Sultanate was in a precarious state throughout the 300 years of its existence, i.e. its political fortunes rose and fell as and when the Sultan was driven out of his erstwhile capital by the Dutch, the Achinese, the Bugis and other foes. They misrepresented it as an argument that the Sultanate had somehow disappeared. They avoided answering our argument in the context of the Malay concept of sovereignty based on the allegiance of subjects and not on territory. We said that this state of affairs meant that it would be difficult, if not impossible, to show that it had sovereignty over Pedra Branca (which was not inhabited until the British took possession of it). They repeatedly stressed their contention that Britain's right to Pedra Branca was only that of the operator of a lighthouse. They argued that there was no need for Johor to protest against any of Britain's activities on the island because Johor had given Britain consent to build the lighthouse.

Malaysia tried very hard to argue before the Court that the whole case hinged on a single issue, that is, whether Pedra Branca was *terra nullius* in 1847 when Singapore took possession of the island, and that the subsequent activities of Singapore on and in relation to the island were irrelevant. Singapore would not be cribbed and cabined in that fashion as her case based on *effectivites*, that is, state activities, was so overwhelming that it was practically conclusive against Malaysia. Given the parlous state of its arguments, Malaysia's Agent tried to influence the judges by insinuating that Singapore had concealed from the Court the missing letter of 1844. He also alleged that Singapore had subverted the long established arrangement reached between Johor and Britain, whereby the British had given permission to build and operate a lighthouse on Pedra Branca (which was the very issue that Malaysia had to prove). Even more disturbing, one of Malaysia's international Counsel reiterated the Co-Agent's insinuation that Singapore had concealed the missing 1844 letter. The Co-Agent went further to accuse Singapore of seeking to establish a maritime domain around Pedra Branca, with militaristic ambitions, and that Singapore's naval presence had caused political tension in the area. The Co-Agent's scare-mongering would have been frightening but for Singapore's realisation that it was par for the course.

Drama in the Court Room

On Friday, 16 November 2007, when Malaysia's international Counsel, Professor Nicholas Schrijver, was speaking, Sir Elihu Lauterpacht fainted and slumped in his chair. This caused quite a sensation in the Court, which had to adjourn for about 15 minutes after efforts were made by a number of people to resuscitate him. An ambulance was summoned and Sir Elihu was taken to a hospital for observation and treatment. After a few days, Sir Elihu recovered and returned to the Court on 20 November 2007 to make his final pitch for Malaysia, although at one point it was rumoured that he would either not appear in Court or would not plead.

On Friday, 23 November, when the Singapore Agent arrived at the Peace Palace at about 2.45pm, he was surprised to be greeted by the Acting President, Judge Awn Shawkat Al-Khasawneh who asked to discuss a delicate matter with him. The Acting President informed him that Sir Elihu had requested the Registrar to expunge from the Court's verbatim record of the proceedings any reference to Sir Elihu's having fainted in Court. The Registrar had reported this request to the Acting President and he was of the view that the request could not be acceded to as the record was accurate and had recorded what had actually happened. He asked our Agent whether he agreed with his view, to which our Agent said yes, whereupon the Acting President asked our Agent to accompany him to see Sir Elihu.

They entered the Malaysia Party Room and were greeted by the Malaysian delegation, some of whom must have wondered what the Singapore Agent was doing in their room. The Foreign Minister of Malaysia, Dato Seri Syed Hamid Albar was also in the room. The Acting President explained the position to him and why the Court could not accede to Sir Elihu's request. The Minister agreed and the three of them then walked over to Sir Elihu, who was seated at a desk near the window, to inform him of the decision. Sir Elihu accepted the decision.

A Busy Weekend

The Singapore delegation spent the weekend, 17 and 18 November, strategising and working on our written pleadings for the second round, which extended over two days. Our international Counsel felt strongly that apart from legal rebuttals, Singapore had to deal robustly with the baseless insinuations by Malaysia concerning Singapore's conduct. It was agreed that it would be best for Jayakumar to do this with a powerful statement at the start of the second round. He would be followed by Chao Hick Tin, Chan Sek Keong and Brownlie. On the second day, Bundy would lead off, followed by Malintoppi, Pellet, with the Agent making the concluding statement and final submissions.

CHAPTER 11

THE SECOND ROUND

Day 1: 19 November 2007

Singapore was allocated the mornings of 19 and 20 November to reply to Malaysia's arguments and allegations against Singapore made to the Court in the first round. Jayakumar fired the first salvo. He made a strong speech, firmly dismissing Malaysia's Co-Agent's allegations as baseless, mischievous and designed to influence the Court in its consideration of Singapore's case. He did not mince his words but they were spoken not out of anger but of disappointment and regret that such tactics were resorted to. Jayakumar dealt with the following:

- An insinuation that Singapore may have withheld the 1844 letter from the Court;

- The allegation that Singapore is subverting the existing legal order and that stability in the region will be affected if sovereignty over Pedra Branca is awarded to Singapore;

- An attribution of sinister motives to Singapore;

- An accusation that Singapore moved its navy belatedly to Pedra Branca and used aggressive methods to assert Singapore's claim; and

- A gratuitous offer to continue to respect Singapore's right to operate the lighthouse should Malaysia win the case.

Chao's Speech

Chao Hick Tin gave a good re-statement of our position on Middle Rocks and South Ledge as forming a legally indivisible group with Pedra Branca. The bulk of his speech was devoted to showing the grievous mistake that Malaysia had made in producing the misleading photograph which it had purported to lift from a recently established website.[45]

Chan's and Pellet's Speeches

Sek Keong then responded to Malaysia's attempt to refute his earlier argument that Johor could not have original historic title to Pedra Branca, since it was an uninhabited island and the Malay concept of sovereignty was based on the allegiance of the people. He rejected Malaysia's attempt to interpret the Anglo-Dutch Treaty as dividing territories instead of spheres of influence. He demonstrated from the contents of Sultan Abdul Rahman's 1825 letter of donation to his brother, Sultan Hussain of Singapore, that he had retained all islands in the sea when he "gave" all his mainland territory to Sultan Hussain. Hence, even on the assumption that the Sultanate had an original title to Pedra Branca (and Singapore had tried to prove that this was not the case), Malaysia could not have inherited Pedra Branca from the Sultanate. He emphasised to the Court that Malaysia's lack of original title was the source and origin of Malaysia's 1953 letter disclaiming ownership over Pedra Branca.

Pellet supplemented Sek Keong's speech by arguing that there was no document or activity by Johor of evidential value to show that Johor had any original title to Pedra Branca. He dismissed Malaysia's argument that Johor had given permission to build the lighthouse on Pedra Branca as completely baseless.

---

[45] Refer to "Mysterious Photograph of Pedra Branca" — Chapter 10.

Bundy's Speech

Bundy's speech focused on Singapore's post-1851 *effectivites*. He told the Court that should it find that the title to Pedra Branca was indeterminate in 1851, and that Singapore's continuous and substantial *effectivites* stood in sharp contrast to Malaysia's complete lack of *effectivites*.

Day 2: 20 November 2007

On the second and final day of round two, the speakers were Bundy, Malintoppi, Pellet and the Agent.

Bundy continued with his speech on *effectivites*. His punch line was: "Indeed, if Malaysia's thesis of the case is accepted, it would produce an unprecedented result — it would be the first time that sovereignty over disputed territory would be found to lie with a party which never carried out a single sovereign act on the actual territory in dispute at any time."

Malintoppi's Speech

Malintoppi sought to demolish the five rather inconsequential episodes of Malaysia's alleged sovereign activities. She also rebutted Malaysia's argument on third state practice. She argued that, on the basis of case law, the Court should attach weight to the six Malaysian maps which attributed Pedra Branca to Singapore, as admissions against Malaysia's interest.

Pellet's Speech

Pellet rejected Malaysia's attempt to downplay the 1953 letter. He argued that, at a minimum, it confirmed Johor's failure to maintain its original title, if it ever had one. In a final blow against Malaysia, Pellet compared the present case to the case of Sipadan and Ligitan. He said that Malaysia had won the Sipadan case, based on *effectivites* which were much more modest than those of Singapore in this case.

The Court in session (Source: Ministry of Foreign Affairs, Singapore)

Agent's Concluding Statement and Final Submissions

The Agent took the Court methodically through the ten key points of Singapore's case. He explained to the Court that all our arguments fitted together like the pieces of a puzzle. All of Singapore's actions were consistent with that of a state which had sovereignty over Pedra Branca. In contrast, all of Malaysia's actions and inactions were consistent with that of a state which had no title to Pedra Branca.

Malaysia's Second Round: 23 and 24 November 2007

Malaysia's Foreign Minister was in Court to give moral support to his delegation. He did not, however, plead on behalf of Malaysia.

We were disappointed that Malaysia was not gracious enough to withdraw her baseless insinuation that Singapore had withheld the 1844 letter from the Court and other allegations concerning

Singapore's intention if Pedra Branca were adjudged to belong to Singapore. Neither did her Counsel explain where Malaysia had obtained the photograph nor apologise or express any regret to the Court for introducing the misleading photograph. We were surprised at these tactics they adopted in their efforts to win the case. As Jayakumar told the Court:

> *"Every State which appears before this honourable Court in a dispute would of course do all it can to persuade this Court to decide in its favour. That is perfectly legitimate. However, we should seek to win by stating objective facts and submitting persuasive legal arguments, and not by resorting to unfounded political statements and making insinuations damaging to the integrity of the opposite party".*[46]

Malaysian Attorney-General's New Argument

Since Malaysia had the last say, it would be unfair for her to raise a new and unpleaded point with full knowledge that Singapore would have no opportunity to respond to it. However, in his speech, the Malaysian Attorney-General did raise a new point and argument on the 1953 disclaimer. He contended that the Acting State Secretary of Johor did not have the capacity to provide a disclaimer or to renounce title under the Johor Agreement of 1948 and the Federation of Malaya Agreement of 1948 as it involved foreign affairs, a subject matter which had been delegated by the individual States to the Federal Government. This was a new argument because in all three rounds of the written pleadings, Malaysia never disputed Singapore's assertion that the Johor State Secretary had the power to make the disclaimer. During the first round of the oral proceedings, Sir Elihu mentioned, in passing, that the State Secretary "lacked the capacity to <u>dispose</u> of Johor's territory". This is, of course, an entirely different argument from that advanced by the Malaysian Attorney-General in the second round.

---

[46] CR 2007/28, 19 November 2007, p. 18, para. 32 (Jayakumar).

The Singapore delegation was angry and dismayed with Malaysia's unfair tactic of bringing up a new argument in the second round, knowing that we could not respond. We brainstormed with Counsel: was there any way we could respond or send word to the Court that we wanted to respond? They said no and asked us to accept the position. We said that this was an impossible situation and we could not believe that in such an important matter as a dispute on territorial sovereignty, the party that might be severely disadvantaged could have no recourse to the rules of natural justice. We were advised to hope for the best. At one point in the discussion, Chan Sek Keong asked Brownlie to pray hard that one of the Judges would have seen the injustice of the situation and would rectify it by asking the appropriate question in order to allow us to respond.

23 November 2007

November 23rd was the final day. It is customary for the judges to take a 20-minute coffee break during the proceedings. On the afternoon of 23 November, the coffee break was much longer than the customary 20 minutes. The Singapore delegation noticed the longer than usual adjournment and surmised that the judges must be in conference to decide whether they should pose some questions to the two parties. Jayakumar offered a wager of 10 Euros that the Court would ask us a question about the new argument raised by the Malaysian Attorney-General. Several colleagues took Jayakumar's bet and lost, but it was a bet they were happy to lose!

Our Prayers Answered: Judge Kenneth Keith Asks a Question

At the end of the proceedings, the Acting President announced that Judge Kenneth Keith wished to pose a question to Singapore. The question was:

What response, if any, does Singapore wish to make in reply to the submission made yesterday by the Attorney-General of Malaysia, expressly by reference to provisions of the Johor Agreement of 1948 and the Federation of Malaya Agreement of 1948, that the Acting State Secretary of Johor "was definitely not authorised" and did not have "the legal capacity to write the 1953 letter, or to renounce, disclaim or confirm title of any part of the territories of Johor"?

Our hope and prayers had been answered.

Another Question by Judge Keith

On 16 November 2007, Judge Keith had posed a question to both Malaysia and Singapore. The question was:

The appeal to the Judicial Committee of the Privy Council from the decision of the Pitcairn Court of Appeal, referred to by the Parties, was dismissed on 30 October 2006. The reference is Christian & ors v. The Queen [2007] 2WLR 120, [2006] UKPC 47.

The question for each Party is as follows: is there anything in the judgments of the Judicial Committee of significance for the present case?

What was the significance of this question? The significance was that Malaysia had argued forcefully that British practice required that there be a formal act of acquisition such as a declaration or the planting of the British flag. In the Pitcairn Island case, the Court of Appeal of New Zealand in dismissing the appeal did not overrule the judgment of the lower court which held that the British Crown had acquired sovereignty over Pitcairn Island, over a period of time and without a formal act such as a declaration or the planting of a flag. Similarly, the British had not done any such act with respect to Pedra Branca. Singapore's answer to this question was prepared overnight and discussed with international Counsel at The Hague. The final text of our reply was, however, sent after our return to Singapore.[47]

Back to Work

The Singapore delegation left The Hague, via Amsterdam, for Singapore, leaving behind Pang Khang Chau to prepare a first draft reply to Judge Keith's question on the capacity of the Johor State Secretary for consideration by the team in Singapore. Although we were all exhausted, we had no choice but to return to work immediately, composing our reply to Judge Keith's question. The deadline was two weeks. Back in Singapore, the team re-assembled and met daily under Chan Sek Keong's chairmanship. Additional research was done immediately. Once again, the NAS was asked to help. Our draft reply was discussed, revised, refined until everyone was satisfied.

Malaysia responded at some length to Singapore's reply to Judge Keith's question on the capacity of the Johor State Secretary on 7 December 2007. Surprisingly, Malaysia, in her reply to Judge Keith's question, again introduced new material in the form of five new documents. We were put in a dilemma as to whether we should send another unsolicited reply to the Court. After receiving advice from international Counsel, we decided that we would write to the Registrar to apprise him of this new development and at the same time comment on three of the new documents, which were material to the question posed by Judge Keith.

Role of the Media

The Pedra Branca case received a great deal of media and public attention, both in Malaysia and Singapore. The media, on both sides of the causeway, started reporting on the case in the weeks

---

[47] The texts of Singapore's response to the two questions are at Annexes A and B.

S Jayakumar thanks the team and international Counsel at
dinner after the oral pleadings (Source: Ministry of
Foreign Affairs, Singapore)

leading up to the oral proceedings. Malaysia sent a very large
contingent of people, both from the print and electronic media,
to The Hague. In the case of Singapore, *The Straits Times* sent
a senior journalist, Lydia Lim, and Channel NewsAsia sent an
experienced reporter, May Wong.

We are pleased to say that, on the whole, both the Singapore
and Malaysia media reported the oral proceedings factually
and in a balanced manner. In fact, during the second week of
the oral proceedings, when Malaysia was presenting its case,
The Straits Times did such a good job reporting on Malaysia's
arguments that we were told that some Singaporeans were
betting 60:40 that Malaysia would win the case! We did not
know whether the punters had changed the odds after reading
Singapore's presentations in the second round in the third week,
but we were confident that we had answered all of Malaysia's
points and left them with nothing substantial to say in their
final speeches, except to spring a new argument on us.

CHAPTER 12

THE JUDGMENT AND OUR REFLECTIONS

Court Notifies Us of the Date of Judgment

Weeks of speculation as to when the judgment would be handed down came to an end on 29 April 2008, when the Court notified us that the judgment would be delivered at 10.00 am on Friday, 23 May 2008.

What was the mood on our side? We were quietly confident because we believed that we had presented a stronger legal case.

As Chan Sek Keong had told us at the conclusion of the hearings: based on his experience as a practising lawyer, an Attorney-General and a Judge, he would be truly astonished if the Court were to give judgment in favour of Malaysia.

Also, as Bundy told the Court on 20 November 2007:

"Indeed, if Malaysia's thesis of the case is accepted, it would produce an unprecedented result: it would be the first time that sovereignty over disputed territory would be found to lie with a party which never carried out a single sovereign act on the actual territory in dispute at any time."

However, we reminded ourselves that there was always an element of uncertainty and that we should be mentally prepared for the scenario where the judgment may be given against us.

After all, there were 16 Judges (including the two Judges *ad hoc*) and they were from 16 countries with different legal backgrounds. Unlike the proceedings in some domestic courts, the ICJ judges do not intervene in the oral hearings and there had been only two questions posed by one of the Judges, namely Judge Keith. It was very difficult to fathom the attitude of the Court.

Jayakumar, Chan Sek Keong and Tommy Koh to be at the ICJ to Receive the Judgment

Jayakumar discussed with Sek Keong and Tommy whether we should all make an effort to be present at The Hague for the delivery of the judgment. It was not critical for all of us to be present. It would be sufficient for the Agent (Tommy), with the co-Agent, our Ambassador in Brussels, Anil Kumar, to be present. Nevertheless, the three of us decided that we would make the trip. This would again show the importance that Singapore attached to the case, and also demonstrate our support for the ICJ process. Furthermore, because we had been involved with the case for so many years, we felt we should see it through to the very end, whatever the outcome.

Preparing for Different Scenarios and Working with Malaysians in Advance of the Verdict

The new Foreign Minister of Malaysia, Datuk Seri Dr Rais Yatim, made his introductory visit to Singapore on 17 April 2008. When he and Foreign Minister George Yeo met the press, George Yeo summed up their discussion on Pedra Branca reiterating that that both sides would honour the ICJ ruling. George Yeo said:

> "… *both of us had agreed that if Malaysia were to win, then we will congratulate Malaysia. Foreign Minister Rais Yatim told me if Singapore were to win, he will congratulate Singapore and that whatever the decision, we will accept it*

Singapore Foreign Minister George Yeo with Malaysian Foreign Minister Rais Yatim at the Ministry of Foreign Affairs, Singapore
(Source: Ministry of Foreign Affairs, Singapore)

and it will not affect bilateral relations. The lighthouse will continue to provide [a] valuable facility to all navigators so nothing should change and this is the common position that we take and that we are proudly happy to declare to all Malaysians and Singaporeans."

Meanwhile, MFA led an inter-agency team to think through the various post-judgment scenarios and implementation measures. For example, if the Court found in favour of Malaysia, we would need to discuss with Malaysia details of how both sides would implement the decision. Likewise, if the decision was in our favour, we would still need to engage Malaysia to ensure that there would be no untoward incidents on the ground.

A few weeks before the date of the judgment, at the sidelines of an ASEAN Senior Official's Meeting, Malaysia's Senior Officials' Meeting Leader Rastam Mohd Isa and Singapore's

Senior Officials' Meeting Leader Peter Ho discussed the idea of establishing a mechanism to ensure the smooth implementation of the Court's judgment regardless of which country was awarded sovereignty. Subsequently, the Joint Committee was established and held its first meeting in Kuala Lumpur on 16 May 2008.

Judgment Day

The night before the day of judgment, our Ambassador Anil Kumar hosted dinner for us at a small but cosy Indonesian restaurant in The Hague. We were joined by Brownlie and his wife. Pellet could not attend the hearing as he had other commitments. Bundy and Malintoppi were scheduled to attend but at the last minute could not make the trip. The mood among team members was upbeat, but laced with a tinge of realism that we must be prepared for surprises.

On the morning of the Court hearing, we greeted the Malaysian delegation as we entered the Court including Rais Yatim and his wife. For the first hour of the reading of the judgment, the Singapore delegation was on tenterhooks because the Court gave a blow by blow rejection of our arguments on history and the status of Pedra Branca as *terra nullius*. In fact, the Court accepted Malaysia's arguments on historic title and concluded:

> *"the Court concludes that Malaysia has established to the satisfaction of the Court that as of the time when the British started their preparations for the construction of the lighthouse on Pedra Branca/Pulau Batu Puteh in 1844, this island was under the sovereignty of the Sultan of Johor."*

> *Source: ICJ Judgment, para. 117, p. 36*

Up to that point, the judgment was going very badly for us. Ambassador Anil Kumar's wife Peck See, who was present at the hearing, confided later that she was so worried that she started to pray. We began to breathe a sigh of relief when

The team exchanging views at the party room inside the
Peace Palace prior to the judgment (Source: Ministry of
Foreign Affairs, Singapore)

the Court began to analyse our arguments on *effectivites* and
Malaysia's acquiescence and recognition of Singapore's title to
Pedra Branca.

We knew then that the Court was, in effect, prepared to
consider the alternative argument that "even in that event, that
is to say that Malaysia could somehow show a historic title
over the island, Singapore still possessed sovereignty over Pedra
Branca since Singapore has exercised continuous sovereignty
over the island while Malaysia has done nothing" (*Source: ICJ
Judgment, para. 123, p. 37*).

We always felt we had irrefutable arguments for this
aspect of the case. First, the Court examined the significance
of the 1953 letter of disclaimer. The Court considered the
1953 correspondence and its interpretation to be of "central
importance" for developing the understanding of the two parties'
sovereignty over Pedra Branca. After examining all the facts
and legal arguments concerning this letter, the Court made this
crucial conclusion that:

> *"... it becomes evident that the letter addresses the issue of
> sovereignty over the island. The Court accordingly concludes
> that Johor's reply shows that as of 1953 Johor understood
> that it did not have sovereignty over Pedra Branca/Pulau
> Batu Puteh."*

Source: ICJ Judgment, para. 223, p. 62

The Court next reviewed the subsequent conduct of the UK and Singapore with respect to Pedra Branca. The Court found that some of their activities, such as the investigation of marine accidents, their control over visits, the installation of naval communications equipment, and its reclamation plans, were acts *á titre de souverain* (acts in right of sovereignty). In contrast, the Johor authorities and their successor took no action at all from June 1850 until the critical date. The Court also noted that when Malaysian officials visited the island, they did so with the express permission of Singapore. In addition, the Court took into account the six Malaysian maps attributing ownership of Pedra Branca to Singapore. The Court's next crucial conclusion based on the conduct of the parties was:

> *"that by 1980 sovereignty over Pedra Branca/Pulau Batu Puteh had passed over to Singapore."*

> *Source: ICJ Judgment, para. 276, p. 75*

At this stage, Jayakumar, Tommy Koh and Chan Sek Keong quietly shook hands because we had won on Pedra Branca, which was the central issue of the case. To maintain the decorum of the Court, our delegation refrained from displaying excessive jubilation but there were smiles all around. The Court then went on to give its findings on Middle Rocks and South Ledge. On Middle Rocks, the Court held that the circumstances leading to the passing of title to Singapore over Pedra Branca did not apply to Middle Rocks and therefore, Malaysia's original title to Middle Rocks remains.

On South Ledge, the Court found that there are special problems to be considered because South Ledge, as distinct from Middle Rocks, is a low-tide elevation. The Court noted that International treaty law is silent on the question whether low tide elevations can be considered territory. Nor is the Court aware of a uniform and widespread State practice that might have given rise to a customary rule which unequivocally permits or excludes appropriation of low-tide elevations. In these circumstances, the Court concluded that sovereignty over

The Singapore team at the Court for the ICJ Judgment
(Source: Ministry of Foreign Affairs, Singapore)

South Ledge, as a low tide elevation, belongs to the State in whose territorial waters it is located.

How the Judges Voted

This was how the Judges voted on the three issues.

(a)   The finding *"that sovereignty over Pedra Branca/Pulau Batu Puteh belongs to the Republic of Singapore,"* was by 12 votes to 4.

Judges voting in favour were: Vice President and Acting President Al-Khasawneh (Jordan); Judges Ranjeva (Madagascar), Shi (China), Koroma (Sierra Leone), Buergenthal (USA), Owada (Japan), Tomka (Slovakia), Keith (New Zealand), Sepulveda-Amor (Mexico), Bennouna (Morocco), Skotnikov (Russia); and Judge *ad hoc* Sreenivasa Rao (India).

Judges voting against were: Judges Parra-Aranguren (Venezuela), Simma (Germany), Abraham (France) and Judge *ad hoc* Dugard (South Africa).

(b)   The finding *"that sovereignty over Middle Rocks belongs to Malaysia"* was by 15 votes to 1.

Original copy of the ICJ Judgment with the Seal of the Court
(Source: Ministry of Foreign Affairs, Singapore)

Judges voting in favour were: Vice President and Acting President Al-Khasawneh (Jordon); Judges Ranjeva (Madagascar), Shi (China), Koroma (Sierra Leone), Parra-Aranguren (Venezuela), Buergenthal (USA), Owada (Japan), Simma (Germany), Tomka (Slovakia), Abraham (France), Keith (New Zealand), Sepulveda-Amor (Mexico), Bennouna (Morocco), Skotnikov (Russia); and Judge *ad hoc* Dugard (South Africa).

Judge voting against was: Judge *ad hoc* Sreenivasa Rao (India).

(c)   The finding that *"sovereignty over South Ledge belongs to the State in the territorial waters of which it is located"* was by 15 votes to 1.

Judges voting in favour were: In favour were Vice President and Acting President Al-Khasawneh (Jordon); Judges Ranjeva (Madagascar), Shi (China), Koroma (Sierra Leone), Buergenthal (USA), Owada (Japan), Simma (Germany), Tomka (Slovakia), Abraham (France), Keith (New Zealand), Sepulveda-Amor (Mexico), Bennouna (Morocco), Skotnikov (Russia); Judge *ad hoc* Dugard (South Africa) and Judge *ad hoc* Sreenivasa Rao (India).

Judge voting against was: Parra-Aranguren (Venezuela).

Were We Completely Surprised at this Split Decision?

The day before the judgment our media had carried Tommy Koh's interview on four possible outcomes: (i) all three features belong to Singapore; (ii) all three features belong to Malaysia; (iii) Pedra Branca belongs to Singapore while Middle Rocks and South Ledge belong to Malaysia; (iv) Pedra Branca belongs to Malaysia, while Middle Rocks and South Ledge belong to Singapore. Therefore, this decision was a possibility we had contemplated. Of course, our team was disappointed that all three features were not awarded to Singapore, but given the Court's ruling that we had failed on the *terra nullius* argument, it is not altogether surprising that the Court arrived at this decision.

Immediately after the Court adjourned, we greeted the Malaysian delegation, who congratulated us. In an interview with the international and local media, Jayakumar said:

> "We are pleased with the judgment because the Court has awarded sovereignty over Pedra Branca, which is the main feature in the dispute, to Singapore. Of course, we would have been happier if the Court had awarded all the three features in Singapore's favour, and we have argued before the Court that all these other features were part of Pedra Branca, but the Court has found otherwise and we accept the judgment of the Court."

Doorstop interview by Jayakumar immediately after Judgment
(Source: Ministry of Foreign Affairs, Singapore)

Prime Minister Lee Hsien Loong and Cabinet watching the
live-telecast of the ICJ Judgment in Cabinet room
(Source: Ministry of Information, Communications and the Arts)

Jayakumar on the phone with PM Lee to discuss the outcome of the case (Source: Ministry of Foreign Affairs, Singapore)

PM and Cabinet Followed the Proceedings Closely

Prime Minister Lee Hsien Loong and Cabinet were very keen to keep abreast of the latest developments on the case. Before the team left for The Hague, Prime Minister told Jayakumar that he especially rescheduled the weekly Cabinet meeting on Friday, 23 May, so that all Cabinet Ministers could view the live telecast of the reading of the judgment.

Immediately after the judgment, Jayakumar telephoned Prime Minister who was still chairing the Cabinet meeting. They discussed briefly the Court's judgment. Prime Minister told Jayakumar that he was pleased with the outcome and asked him to thank the members of the team. Later that evening, Prime Minister issued a statement in Singapore:

> *"I am pleased with the result. We fully accept the judgment of the ICJ. I am glad that Malaysia has also consistently said that it will accept the ICJ judgment. This is a good way for*

us to resolve disagreements or problems while maintaining good relations with each other .... I am glad that this problem is now cleared. I will be writing to PM Abdullah to express my thanks to him that both our countries have been able to work together to resolve this problem, and we can now go on to develop our cooperation in many areas, such as the Iskandar Malaysia project.

... I would especially like to thank the Singapore team at The Hague. They did a magnificent job in preparing and presenting our case before the ICJ. DPM Jayakumar, Ambassador Tommy Koh, Chief Justice Chan Sek Keong, our international Counsel, and many officials from our ministries and agencies have worked very hard on this case for a long time — in DPM Jayakumar's case, for 29 years. On behalf of Singaporeans, I thank all of them for their contributions and efforts."

Source: Quote from PM's press statement

The Key Factor for Success: The Importance of Working as a Cohesive Team

What contributed to the successful outcome? The legal arguments? The well written pleadings? The persuasiveness of the oral arguments of all the Singapore team members? The fact that we had very good international Counsel?

Of course, each of these elements was important. In our view, the most important factor was that over the three decades we had been preparing the case, all agencies in Singapore worked closely together. The Pedra Branca story is an excellent illustration of the "whole of Government approach".

Because of the above, the two major drivers of the Singapore team, AGC and MFA, were able to work harmoniously. In addition to AGC and MFA, the team also included representatives of NAS, MPA, MINDEF, especially the Navy, scholars from NUS, the four international Counsel, our history consultants, and others.

The Singapore team (Source: Ministry of Foreign Affairs, Singapore)

It probably helped that the four most senior members of the Singapore team: the Deputy Prime Minister, Chief Justice, Attorney-General and Agent, were very old friends who could work well together.

Several of our international Counsel remarked on the strength of the AGC team. Led by the experienced veteran, Sivakant Tiwari, it was a group of remarkably talented and hard-working international lawyers, consisting of Lionel Yee, Pang Khang Chau, Tan Ken Hwee, Daren Tang and Ong Chin Heng.

The Singapore team was augmented by four international Counsel. What was most satisfying was that the Singaporeans and the non-Singaporeans got along well, bonded and conducted themselves as one team. The fact that the four international Counsel were nationals of four different countries did not create complications.

Singapore's Continued Commitment to Third Party Dispute Settlement

What are our final reflections? Has our first experience of referring a dispute to the ICJ been a positive one? Does the fact that the Court's decision was a split one affect Singapore's commitment to third party dispute settlement? We would say that, on the whole, it has been a positive experience and we have learnt many lessons from it. We are gratified that the Court has awarded sovereignty over Pedra Branca to Singapore. We are, of course, disappointed that the Court did not award sovereignty over the other two marine features to Singapore. However, we accept the judgment of the Court without qualification. It has not changed our commitment to the policy of referring disputes, which cannot be resolved by negotiation, to third party dispute settlement. We will continue to abide by international law and work with other like-minded states to strengthen the rule of law in the world.

* * * * *

ANSWERS TO JUDGES' QUESTIONS

CASE CONCERNING SOVEREIGNTY OVER PEDRA BRANCA/PULAU BATU PUTEH, MIDDLE ROCKS AND SOUTH LEDGE
(MALAYSIA/SINGAPORE)

ANNEX A: RESPONSE OF SINGAPORE TO THE QUESTION POSED BY JUDGE KEITH TO BOTH PARTIES ON 16 NOVEMBER 2007

Question

The appeal to the Judicial Committee of the Privy Council from the decision of the Pitcairn Court of Appeal, referred to by the Parties, was dismissed on 30 October 2006. The reference is *Christian & ors v. The Queen* [2007] 2 WLR 120, [2006] UKPC 47.

The question for each Party is as follows: is there anything in the judgments of the Judicial Committee of significance for the present case?

Response

1   Singapore's answer to the question is that the judgments of the Judicial Committee of the Privy Council are significant in that they did not seek to disturb the statement of the law on British practice on the acquisition of territory made by the Pitcairn Court of Appeal (and cited by Singapore during the oral proceedings[1]). The authority of the Court of Appeal's statement on this matter therefore stands.

2   The Court of Appeal had, after a detailed examination of "the substantial volume of documentary material presented to the

---

[1] CR 2007/21, 7 November 2007, p. 47, paras. 60-61 (Brownlie); CR 2007/23, 9 November 2007, p. 59, para. 19 (Jayakumar); CR 2007/28, 19 November 2007, p. 61, para. 50 (Brownlie).

Court resulting from the industry of counsel,"[2] on "the historical basis relating to the United Kingdom claim of sovereignty over Pitcairn Island and its status as a British settlement, insofar as that can be done from the material"[3], made the following statement of law on British practice at para. 46:

> "It is not necessary to define with accuracy the time at which Pitcairn Island did become a British possession. Sometimes there may be a gradual extension of jurisdiction over a territory, as was recognised in *Attorney General for British Honduras v. Bristowe* (1880) 6 App Cas 143. British Honduras was formally annexed in 1862, but there were grants of land by the Crown made as early as 1817. The Privy Council held that sovereignty was acquired on or before that earlier year. Similarly, *a formal act of acquisition is not required. It is the intention of the Crown, gathered from its own acts and surrounding circumstances*, that determines whether a territory has been acquired for English law purposes. *The same principle applies in the resolution of international disputes as to sovereignty.*"[4] [Emphasis added]

3   This statement of the law was not necessary to the disposal of the appeal. Nonetheless, the statement was a fully considered determination after an extensive examination of the law and the facts in that case and after hearing full arguments. The statement therefore stands as an authoritative statement of English law by the Court of Appeal.

4   The following observations may be made about the statement of the law pronounced by the Court of Appeal:

- It is a fully considered, authoritative statement of the law on British practice.

- It supports Singapore's position that a formal act of acquisition is not required both in British practice and in public international law.

- The statement by the Court of Appeal that "it is not necessary to define with accuracy the time at which Pitcairn Island did become a British possession" supports Singapore's position.

---

[2] 127 *ILR* 232, p. 291, para. 34.
[3] *Ibid.*
[4] *Ibid.*, pp. 294–295, para. 46 (emphasis added).

- The statement is of general application, and is not confined to any specific situation. As such, it is applicable to the situation of Pedra Branca.

- The test laid down in this statement is *"the intention of the Crown, gathered from its own acts and surrounding circumstances"*. Singapore has satisfied this test in the present case, as was explained in Singapore's written pleadings and by Mr Brownlie on behalf of Singapore during the oral proceedings.[5]

Respectfully submitted,

Anil Kumar Nayar
Co-Agent of the Republic of Singapore

---

[5] Memorial of Singapore (MS), pp. 29–87, paras. 5.1–5.113; Counter Memorial of Singapore (CMS), pp. 73–128, paras. 5.1–5.139; Reply of Singapore (RS), pp. 35–94, paras. 3.1–3.134; CR 2007/21, 7 November 2007, pp. 36–69, paras. 12–154 (Brownlie); CR 2007/28, 19 November 2007, pp. 52–61, paras. 8–49 (Brownlie).

CASE CONCERNING SOVEREIGNTY OVER PEDRA BRANCA/PULAU BATU PUTEH, MIDDLE ROCKS AND SOUTH LEDGE
(MALAYSIA/SINGAPORE)

ANNEX B: RESPONSE OF SINGAPORE TO THE QUESTION POSED BY JUDGE KEITH TO SINGAPORE ON 23 NOVEMBER 2007

Question

What response, if any, does Singapore wish to make in reply to the submission made yesterday by the Attorney-General of Malaysia, expressly by reference to provisions of the Johor Agreement of 1948 and the Federation of Malaya Agreement of 1948, that the Acting State Secretary of Johor "was definitely not authorized" and did not have "the legal capacity to write the 1953 letter, or to renounce, disclaim, or confirm title of any part of the territories of Johor"?

Response

1   Singapore notes as a preliminary point that the submission of the Attorney-General of Malaysia is a new argument, presented for the very first time by Malaysia on 22 November 2007.

2   The Court will recall that Singapore's Memorial expressly put the capacity of the Johor State Secretary into issue by asserting unequivocally that "*[h]e had the power to make a disclaimer of title on behalf of Johor*".[6] In all three rounds of written pleadings, Malaysia did not dispute Singapore's assertion that the Johor State Secretary had the power to make the disclaimer.

3   The first time that Malaysia referred to the capacity of the State Secretary in connection with the 1953 letter was in Sir Elihu

---

[6] MS, p. 167, para. 8.15.

Lauterpacht's submission during Malaysia's first round of oral presentation. Sir Elihu mentioned in passing that the State Secretary "*lacked the capacity to _dispose_ of Johor's territory*",[7] which is a completely different argument from that advanced by Malaysia's Attorney-General in the second round. In its second round presentation, Singapore responded to Sir Elihu's argument by a reminder that it is not Singapore's case that the 1953 letter amounted to a cession of territory.[8]

4   The Malaysian Attorney-General's new argument is that the Johore Agreement of 1948 ("Johor Agreement") and the Federation of Malaya Agreement of 1948 ("Federation Agreement") somehow deprived the Johor State Secretary of the capacity to "write the 1953 letter or to renounce, disclaim or confirm title of any part of the territories of Johor".

5   This very late change in Malaysia's position on the capacity of the Johor State Secretary must surely weigh heavily against the credibility and veracity of Malaysia's new argument. This new argument is no more than an attempt to muddy the waters over a very straightforward issue – that a high official of Johor gave an unequivocal, unconditional disclaimer of title to Pedra Branca, i.e., by informing Singapore officially that Johor did not claim ownership of Pedra Branca.

Recapitulation of Malaysia's New Argument

6   Malaysia's new argument is as follows:

(a)   By the Johor Agreement and the Federation Agreement, Johor had no competence to deal with external affairs as it had transferred control over its external affairs to Britain.

(b)   The Acting State Secretary of Johor "undertook himself" to write directly to Singapore in 1953, without the knowledge or consent of the High Commissioner of the Federation (or his Chief Secretary).[9] The way the correspondence was conducted was "procedurally irregular and incorrect".[10]

---

[7] CR 2007/24, 13 November 2007, p. 54, para. 63 (Lauterpacht).

[8] CR 2007/29, 20 November 2007, p. 46, para. 13 (Pellet).

[9] CR 2007/30, 22 November 2007, p. 18, para. 23 (Gani Patail).

[10] *Ibid.*

(c)   The Acting State Secretary of Johor "was definitely not authorized or had the legal capacity to write the 1953 letter, or to renounce, disclaim, or confirm title of any part of the territories of Johor".[11]

The Johor State Secretary had the Capacity to Issue the 1953 Disclaimer

7   The Malaysian Attorney-General's argument is difficult to follow. While it is clear that the argument hinges on the transfer of control over external affairs by Johor to Britain, it is not clear from his argument how this would have deprived the Johor State Secretary of the authority or legal capacity to write the 1953 letter and/or to disclaim title *in the sense or the manner described in the Singapore pleadings.*

8   It is useful to begin by examining the difference between the terminology used by the Malaysian Attorney-General and the terminology used by Singapore. The Malaysian Attorney-General argues that the Johor State Secretary had no capacity to "renounce, disclaim or confirm title to any part of Johor's territory". But that has never been Singapore's argument. Singapore has never argued that Johor renounced title to Pedra Branca for the simple reason that Johor had no title to Pedra Branca to renounce or abandon. As for confirmation of title, it is not Singapore's argument that the Johor State Secretary confirmed Singapore's title to territory. Singapore's argument is simply that, by declaring that Johor did not claim Pedra Branca, the Johor State Secretary's letter had the effect of confirming Singapore's title to Pedra Branca and of confirming that Johor had no title, historic or otherwise, to the island. As for the term "disclaimer of title", Singapore has explained in its Memorial that:

> "8.16   It should be emphasised that it is not Singapore's case that Johor abandoned or relinquished title to Pedra Branca in 1953. *Abandonment* or *relinquishment* of title is possible only if there is a pre-existing title. What Johor did by her 1953 letter was not to renounce title (since she did not have title)

---

[11] CR 2007/30, 22 November 2007, p. 18, para. 22 (Gani Patail).

or a "claim" to ownership, but rather to *pronounce* explicitly that Johor *did not have* a claim to ownership of Pedra Branca. It must also be emphasised that, in the context of Singapore's possession of the island and in the absence of any claim or interest by third States, Johor's disclaimer can only be regarded as an unequivocal recognition of Singapore's title."[12]

As will be explained later, neither the Johor Agreement nor the Federation Agreement precluded the Johor State Secretary from giving such a disclaimer.

9   In his submission, the Malaysian Attorney-General first referred to Clause 3(1) of the Johor Agreement which vested control of Johor's external affairs in the British Crown. The Malaysian Attorney-General then referred to Clause 3(2), under which Johor "*undertakes that, without the knowledge and consent of His Majesty's Government, he will not make any treaty, enter into any engagement, deal in or correspond on political matters with or send envoys to, any foreign State*".

10   Clearly, the phrase "foreign State" in the context of Clause 3(2) did not include Britain. It would be absurd to require Johor to seek Britain's permission to correspond with Britain itself. It follows that, as Singapore was a British colony in 1953, Clause 3 did not prohibit Johor from corresponding with Singapore. Very clearly, nothing turns on the Johor Agreement.

11   Next, the Malaysian Attorney-General referred to Clause 4 of the Federation Agreement which gave Britain control over the external affairs of the Federation. He also referred to the Second Schedule of the Federation Agreement, which set out "External Affairs" as a subject over which the Federation had legislative and executive authority. It is well known that the term "External Affairs" appearing in constitutions of the Commonwealth is imprecise in meaning and has been differently interpreted in different jurisdictions and at different periods of time. The Federation Agreement itself did not define the term "External Affairs", except by way of inclusion of

---

[12] MS, p.167, para. 8.16.

three specific classes of matters as part of external affairs. Under the Federation Agreement, the power to interpret the agreement was vested exclusively in an Interpretation Tribunal set up under Clause 153 of the Federation Agreement. The Interpretation Tribunal was convened only once during the nine years that the Federation Agreement was in operation (1948–1957)[13] and the term "External Affairs" did not come up for consideration on that occasion. In the circumstances, there was no authoritative interpretation of the term "External Affairs" in the Federation Agreement.

12   The Malaysian Attorney-General's argument therefore finds no support in authority. It is also not supported by actual official practice under the Federation Agreement. During the period when the Federation Agreement was in force, Johor officials continued to correspond routinely with their counterparts in Singapore on matters under their charge. Thus, the Johor State Secretary continued to correspond directly with the Singapore Government on matters concerning the supply of water to Singapore.[14] Similarly, the Chief Police Officer of Johor continued to correspond directly with his counterpart in Singapore on cooperative policing of the Johor Strait.[15] Other examples include the Johor Harbour Master and the Johor Controller of Supplies.[16] Evidently, such direct communications between Johor officials and their Singapore counterparts were never regarded as an encroachment on the power of the Federation over "External Affairs".

13   By the same token, the 1953 letter did not encroach on the external affairs power of the Federation. By no stretch of the imagination can the 1953 letter be construed as an exercise of "executive authority" over "External Affairs". J.D. Higham (from the Singapore

---

[13] *Interpretation Tribunal, Federation of Malaya Agreement, 1948* [1950] Malayan Law Reports 35.

[14] Letter from State Secretary, Johor to President, City Council, Singapore dated 27 November 1952.

[15] Letter from the Singapore Deputy Commissioner of Police to the Chief Police Officer, Johor dated 2 July 1948 (CMS Annex 30).

[16] Letter from Harbour Master, Johor to Fishery Officer, Singapore dated 3 September 1949 & Letter from Asst Controller of Supplies, Johor to Ag Deputy Director of Fisheries, Singapore dated 15 October 1953.

Colonial Secretary's office) did not write directly to the Johor State Secretary. He wrote to the British Adviser in Johor and copied his letter to the Chief Secretary of the Federation. Evidently, the Chief Secretary of the Federation did not think that Higham's letter encroached on matters of "External Affairs" over which he had exclusive authority. Otherwise, he would have intervened and assumed the responsibility for replying to Higham's letter.

14   The reaction of the British Adviser was equally telling. Contrary to Malaysia's argument, the Johor State Secretary did not "undert[ake] himself to issue the letter to J. D. Higham".[17] It was the British Adviser who passed Higham's letter on to the Johor State Secretary. Clearly, the British Adviser did not think that the Johor State Secretary lacked the capacity to deal with Higham's inquiry. Similarly, the Johor State Secretary himself did not think that there was anything procedurally wrong about his responding to Higham. Finally, Higham referred the Johor State Secretary's response to the Singapore Attorney-General. Far from pointing out any supposed procedural irregularity, the Singapore Attorney-General agreed with Higham that, on the strength of Johor State Secretary's response, Pedra Branca may be claimed as Singapore territory.

15   The entire process involved four senior British officials on the one side (Higham, the Chief Secretary of the Federation, the British Adviser in Johor and the Singapore Attorney-General) and the highest Johor official on the other side (the Acting State Secretary of Johor). Malaysia has produced no evidence that any one of them thought that Higham's inquiry should be handled by a different official or that the inquiry and response involved a breach of the Johor Agreement or the Federation Agreement. Given that the five persons involved in the correspondence were all high officials, the maxim *omnia praesumuntur rite esse acta* applies to the 1953 letter. The conduct of these officials speaks much louder than any *ex post facto* attempt by Malaysia today to interpret the 1953 letter as being inconsistent with the Johor Agreement or the Federation Agreement.

---

[17] CR 2007/30, 22 November 2007, p. 18, para. 23 (Gani Patail).

The Johor State Secretary's 1953 Letter Remains Binding on Johor even if It Were Issued in a Manner Inconsistent with the Johor Agreement or Federation Agreement

16   The foregoing discussion clearly establishes that the Johor State Secretary's 1953 letter was not issued in breach of the Johor Agreement or the Federation Agreement. However, even assuming for the sake of argument that the Malaysian Attorney-General is right in saying that the 1953 correspondence was "procedurally irregular and incorrect", Singapore's submission is that it would make no difference to the effect of the 1953 letter in international law.

17   The Malaysian Attorney-General's argument did not make clear whether he was relying on the Federation Agreement as a constitution in municipal law or as an international treaty between Britain and Johor. The Federation Agreement is a treaty between Britain and nine Malay States, including Johor. However, it may also be regarded as a constitutional document in municipal law.[18] On either basis, the effect of the 1953 letter in international law remains unchanged.

The Federation Agreement as Treaty

18   Despite transferring control of its defence and external affairs to Britain, it is an undisputed fact that Johor was a sovereign State during the period 1948 to 1957, when the Federation Agreement was in force.[19] The sovereign status of Johor is clear from Clause 15 of the Johor Agreement and Clause 155 of the Federation Agreement. It was also confirmed by the decision of the Privy Council in 1952 in the case of *Sultan of Johor v Tunku Abubakar*.[20]

---

[18] *See* Roberts-Wray, *Commonwealth and Colonial Law* (1966) which described the Federation Agreement as "the new Constitution" (p. 717). *See also* Allen, Stockwell & Wright (eds.), *A Collection of Treaties and Other Documents Affecting the States of Malaysia 1761–1963* (1981), which commented that the Federation Agreement was "more than an agreement. It was a formal constitution for the new Federation ..." (p. 98).

[19] In his speech, the Malaysian Attorney-General noted that Singapore has stated in no uncertain terms that Johor was a sovereign State in 1953 and made no attempt to dispute Singapore's statement. (CR 2007/30, 22 November 2007, p. 14, para. 7).

[20] *Sultan of Johor v Tunku Abubakar* [1952] Appeal Cases 318 (Judgment of the Privy Council of 22 April 1952) (Malaysia has also referred to other British cases confirming Johor's sovereignty, such as *Mighell v Sultan of Johor* [1894] 1 QB 149.).

19   Since the Federation Agreement was a treaty between sovereign States, the Malaysian Attorney-General's argument amounts to an assertion that Johor had acted in breach of her treat(ies) with Britain. If indeed, such a breach had occurred, *quod non*, it would be up to the other treaty party to object to the breach. The facts show that Britain did not object to the "breach" but in fact adopted it – the Attorney-General of the British Colony of Singapore reacted by agreeing with Higham that "we can claim Pedra Branca as Singapore territory".[21] If indeed, Johor had committed such a breach, *quod non*, it was not open to Johor (or Malaysia as Johor's successor) to plead her own wrong, i.e., a breach of a treaty with Britain, against Britain to resile from the unequivocal, unconditional disclaimer which Johor had given to Singapore, a British colony. As stated by the Permanent Court in its Advisory Opinion on *Jurisdiction of the Danzig Courts*:

> "Poland could not avail herself of an objection which … would amount to relying upon the non-fulfillment of an obligation imposed upon her by an international agreement."[22]

The Federation Agreement as a Municipal Constitution

20   If the Federation Agreement were viewed as a municipal constitutional document then, following the decision in the *Eastern Greenland* case, it does not matter what municipal limitations there were on the powers of the Johor State Secretary, as long as it is established that the 1953 letter was "in regard to a question falling within his province".[23] The Permanent Court in *Eastern Greenland* did not inquire into Norway's argument that Norwegian constitutional law did not authorize the Foreign Minister to make the declaration. Instead, the Court focused on the character of the act in question and the functions of the official involved.

21   Given that Johor was a sovereign State between 1948 and 1957 with its own territory, it would certainly be within its competence

---

[21] Internal Memorandum from the Colonial Secretary, Singapore to the Attorney-General, Singapore, and reply, 1[2 sic] October 1953 (Memorial of Malaysia Annex 70).

[22] *Jurisdiction of the Danzig Courts*, Advisory Opinion (1928) P.C.I.J. Reports, Ser. B. No. 15, at pp. 26-27.

[23] *Legal Status of Eastern Greenland Case* (Denmark v. Norway), Judgment (1933) P.C.I.J.Reports, Ser. A/B, No. 53, at p.71.

to make inquiries into the extent of its territory. Indeed, Johor was in the best position to know the extent of its own territory. It was clearly within the province of the State Secretary to make and respond to inquiries on such matters. The 1949 State of Johor Annual Report described the Johor State Secretary as "the Government's official spokesman"[24] and further recorded that:

> "The State Secretary who is appointed by H.H. the Sultan is the Principal Officer in Charge of the Administration *of the Government*. Heads of State Departments, including District Officers and Administrative Officers, *are directly responsible to the State Secretary* for the proper conduct of *all matters* affecting their departments."[25] [Emphasis added]

The Johor State Secretary was obviously in a better position than the Chief Secretary of the Federation to know the extent of Johor's territory and to give an answer in that respect. The British Adviser stated expressly that Higham's inquiry "*should, in the British Adviser's opinion, have been addressed*" to the Johor State Secretary.[26] Indeed, all five senior officials involved were of the view that the 1953 correspondence fell within the State Secretary's province.

Conclusion

22   The Malaysian Attorney-General's argument concerning lack of capacity is devoid of merit and completely irrelevant. Singapore has shown that the writing of the 1953 letter did not contravene the Johor Agreement or the Federation Agreement. Certainly, the relevant officials at the time (both British and Johorean) did not think there was anything "procedurally irregular and incorrect" about the way the disclaimer came to be issued. But, as explained in paragraphs 16 to 21 above, even if the procedures followed by the Johor State Secretary were somehow inconsistent with the

---

[24] *State of Johore Annual Report for 1949* (written by Dato Wan Idris bin Ibrahim, Ag. Mentri Besar [*i.e.*, *Chief Minister*], Johore, printed by Government Printing Department, Johore), at p. 60.

[25] *Ibid. at* p. 61.

[26] Letter from Turner J.D. (Secretary to the British Adviser, Johor) to the Colonial Secretary, Singapore, received on 18 June 1953 (MS Annex 95).

Johor Agreement or the Federation Agreement, that would not in any way diminish the effect of the 1953 letter in international law and its significance as an admission that Johor did not have title to Pedra Branca.

23   The 1953 letter is clear evidence that Johor did not have title to Pedra Branca. It was a solemn declaration by the highest official of the Johor Government given to the Colonial Secretary of Singapore, after he had made ample and extensive inquiries (he took three months to reply). He came to the conclusion that "*the Johore Government does not claim ownership of Pedra Branca*". It was not a one-off mistake as Malaysia now very belatedly alleges without proof. This reply is consistent with all that has gone on before and after. It is consistent with Malaysia's inability to produce any evidence of a transmitted original title. It is consistent with the complete absence of any public assertion of sovereignty over Pedra Branca by Johor (and its successor, Malaysia) before 1979. It is consistent with the fact that neither Johor/Malaysia nor Britain/Singapore once mentioned any alleged "permission" granted by Johor during the 130-year period between 1847 and 1979. It is consistent with the series of official maps published by Malaysia attributing Pedra Branca to Singapore, and with the many other acts on the part of Malaysia recognizing Singapore's sovereignty over Pedra Branca. Malaysia cannot now attempt to disown the 1953 letter on the pretext of lack of authority and capacity on the part of the State Secretary of Johor.

Respectfully submitted,

Anil Kumar Nayar
Co-Agent of the Republic of Singapore

SUMMARY OF THE JUDGMENT

INTERNATIONAL COURT OF JUSTICE
Peace Palace, Carnegieplein 2, 2517 KJ The Hague, Netherlands
Tel.: +31 (0)70 302 2323 Fax: +31 (0)70 364 9928
Website: www.icj-cij.org

Summary 2008/1
23 May 2008

ANNEX C: SOVEREIGNTY OVER PEDRA BRANCA/ PULAU BATU PUTEH, MIDDLE ROCKS AND SOUTH LEDGE (MALAYSIA/SINGAPORE)

SUMMARY OF THE JUDGMENT OF 23 MAY 2008

Chronology of the procedure and submissions of the Parties
(paras. 1-15)

By joint letter dated 24 July 2003, Malaysia and Singapore notified to the Registrar a Special Agreement between the two States, signed at Putrajaya on 6 February 2003 and having entered into force on 9 May 2003. In that Special Agreement they requested the Court to determine whether sovereignty over Pedra Branca/Pulau Batu Puteh, Middle Rocks and South Ledge belongs to Malaysia or Singapore.

Each of the Parties duly filed a Memorial, Counter-Memorial and Reply within the time-limits fixed by the Court, having regard to the provisions of the Special Agreement concerning written pleadings. The Special Agreement provided for the possible filing of a fourth pleading by each of the Parties. However, by a joint letter dated 23 January 2006, the Parties informed the Court that they had agreed that it was not necessary to exchange Rejoinders.

Since the Court included upon the Bench no judge of the nationality of either of the Parties, each Party proceeded to exercise the right conferred by Article 31, paragraph 3, of the Statute to choose a judge ad hoc to sit in the case: Malaysia chose Mr. Christopher John Robert Dugard and Singapore Mr. Sreenivasa Rao Pemmaraju.

Prior to her election as President of the Court, Judge Higgins, referring to Article 17, paragraph 2, of the Statute, recused herself from participating in the case. It therefore fell upon the Vice-President,

Judge Al-Khasawneh, to exercise the functions of the presidency for the purposes of the case, in accordance with Article 13, paragraphs 1 and 2, of the Rules of Court.

Public hearings were held from 6 to 23 November 2007.

Geography, general historical background and history of the dispute (paras. 16-36)

Geography (paras. 16-19)

The Court first describes the geographical context of the dispute.

Pedra Branca/Pulau Batu Puteh is a granite island, measuring 137 m long, with an average width of 60 m and covering an area of about 8,560 sq m at low tide. It is situated at the eastern entrance of the Straits of Singapore, at the point where the latter open up into the South China Sea. Pedra Branca/Pulau Batu Puteh is located at 1° 19' 48" N and 104° 24' 27" E. It lies approximately 24 nautical miles to the east of Singapore, 7.7 nautical miles to the south of the Malaysian state of Johor and 7.6 nautical miles to the north of the Indonesian island of Bintan. The names Pedra Branca and Batu Puteh mean "white rock" in Portuguese and Malay respectively. On the island stands Horsburgh lighthouse, which was erected in the middle of the nineteenth century.

Middle Rocks and South Ledge are the two maritime features closest to Pedra Branca/Pulau Batu Puteh. Middle Rocks is located 0.6 nautical miles to the south and consists of two clusters of small rocks about 250 m apart that are permanently above water and stand 0.6 to 1.2 m high. South Ledge, at 2.2 nautical miles to the south-south-west of Pedra Branca/Pulau Batu Puteh, is a rock formation only visible at low tide. [See sketch-map No. 2]

General historical background (paras. 20-29)

The Court then gives an overview of the complex historical background of the dispute between the Parties (only parts of which are referred to below).

The Sultanate of Johor was established following the capture of Malacca by the Portuguese in 1511. By the mid-1600s the Netherlands had wrested control over various regions in the area from Portugal. In 1795, the British established rule over several Dutch possessions in the Malay archipelago, but in 1814 returned the former Dutch possessions in the Malay archipelago to the Netherlands.

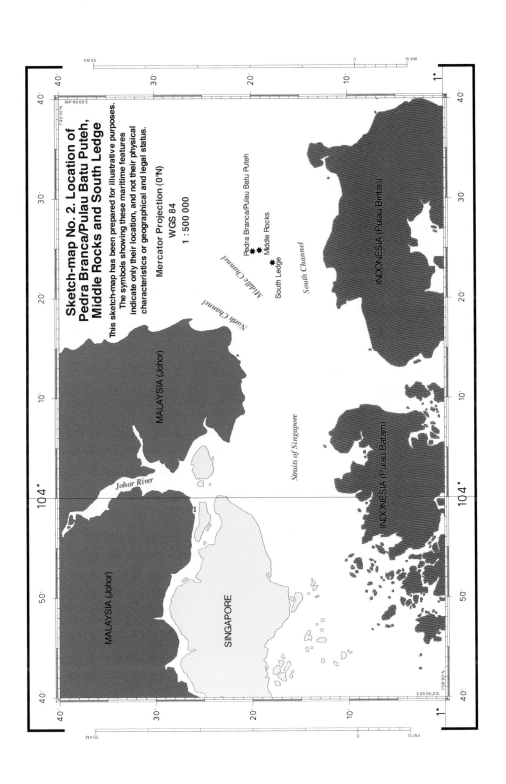

Sketch-map No. 2. Location of Pedra Branca/Pulau Batu Puteh, Middle Rocks and South Ledge

This sketch-map has been prepared for illustrative purposes. The symbols showing these maritime features indicate only their location, and not their physical characteristics or geographical and legal status.

Mercator Projection (0°N)

WGS 84

1 : 500 000

Pedra Branca/Pulau Batu Puteh
Middle Rocks
South Ledge

North Channel
Middle Channel
South Channel

MALAYSIA (Johor)

MALAYSIA (Johor)

Johor River

SINGAPORE

Straits of Singapore

INDONESIA (Pulau Bintan)

INDONESIA (Pulau Batam)

In 1819 a British "factory" (trading station) was established on Singapore island (which belonged to Johor) by the East India Company, acting as an agent of the British Government in various British possessions. This exacerbated the tension between the United Kingdom and the Netherlands arising out of their competing colonial ambitions in the region. On 17 March 1824 a treaty was signed between the two colonial Powers. As a consequence of this Treaty, one part of the Sultanate of Johor fell within the British sphere of influence while the other fell within the Dutch sphere of influence.

On 2 August 1824 a Treaty of Friendship and Alliance (hereinafter "the Crawfurd Treaty") was signed between the East India Company and the Sultan of Johor and the Temenggong (a Malay high-ranking official) of Johor, providing for the full cession of Singapore to the East India Company, along with all islands within 10 geographical miles of Singapore.

Since the death of Sultan Mahmud III of Johor in 1812, his two sons had claimed the succession to the Johor Sultanate. The United Kingdom had recognized as the heir the elder son Hussein (who was based in Singapore), whereas the Netherlands had recognized as the heir the younger son Abdul Rahman (who was based in Riau, present day Pulau Bintan in Indonesia). On 25 June 1825 Sultan Abdul Rahman sent a letter to his elder brother in which he "donated" to him the part of the lands assigned to Sultan Hussein in accordance with the 1824 Anglo-Dutch Treaty.

Between March 1850 and October 1851 a lighthouse was constructed on Pedra Branca/Pulau Batu Puteh.

In 1867 the Straits Settlements, a grouping of East India Company territories established in 1826 consisting, inter alia, of Penang, Singapore and Malacca, became a British crown colony. In 1885 the British Government and the State of Johor concluded the Johor Treaty, which gave the United Kingdom overland trade and transit rights through the State of Johor and responsibility for its foreign relations, as well as providing for British protection of its territorial integrity.

The Straits Settlements were dissolved in 1946; that same year the Malayan Union was created, comprising part of the former Straits Settlements (excluding Singapore), the Federated Malay States and five Unfederated Malay States (including Johor). From 1946, Singapore was administered as a British Crown Colony in its own right. In 1948 the Malayan Union became the Federation of Malaya, a grouping of British colonies and Malay States under the protection of the British.

The Federation of Malaya gained independence from Britain in 1957, with Johor as a constituent state of the Federation. In 1958 Singapore became a self-governing colony. In 1963 the Federation of Malaysia was established, formed by the merger of the Federation of Malaya with the former British colonies of Singapore, Sabah and Sarawak. In 1965 Singapore left the Federation and became a sovereign and independent State.

History of the dispute (paras. 30-36)

The Court notes that, on 21 December 1979 Malaysia published a map entitled "Territorial Waters and Continental Shelf Boundaries of Malaysia" (hereinafter "the 1979 map"). The map depicted the island of Pedra Branca/Pulau Batu Puteh as lying within Malaysia's territorial waters. By a diplomatic Note dated 14 February 1980 Singapore rejected Malaysia's "claim" to Pedra Branca/Pulau Batu Puteh and requested that the 1979 map be corrected. This led to an exchange of correspondence and subsequently to a series of intergovernmental talks in 1993–1994, which did not bring a resolution of the matter. During the first round of talks in February 1993 the question of the appurtenance of Middle Rocks and South Ledge was also raised. In view of the lack of progress in the bilateral negotiations, the Parties agreed to submit the dispute for resolution by the International Court of Justice.

The Court recalls that in the context of a dispute related to sovereignty over land, the date upon which the dispute crystallized is of significance. In the view of the Court, it was on 14 February 1980, the time of Singapore's protest in response to Malaysia's publication of the 1979 map, that the dispute as to sovereignty over Pedra Branca/Pulau Batu Puteh crystallized. With regard to sovereignty over Middle Rocks and South Ledge, the Court finds that the dispute crystallized on 6 February 1993, when Singapore referred to these maritime features in the context of its claim to Pedra Branca/Pulau Batu Puteh during bilateral discussions between the Parties.

Sovereignty over Pedra Branca/Pulau Batu Puteh (paras. 37-277)

Positions of the Parties (paras. 37-42)

Malaysia states in its written pleadings that it "has an original title to Pulau Batu Puteh of long standing. Pulau Batu Puteh is, and has always been, part of the Malaysian State of Johor. Nothing has happened to displace Malaysia's sovereignty over it. Singapore's presence on the island for the sole purpose of constructing and maintaining a lighthouse there — with the permission of the territorial sovereign — is insufficient to vest sovereignty in it." Malaysia further says that the island "could not at any relevant time be considered as terra nullius and hence susceptible to acquisition through occupation".

Singapore claims that "the selection of Pedra Branca as the site for building of the lighthouse with the authorization of the British Crown", a process which started in 1847, "constituted a classic taking of possession à titre de souverain". According to Singapore, title to the island was acquired by the British Crown in accordance with the legal principles of that time and has since "been maintained by the British Crown and its lawful successor, the Republic of Singapore". While in Singapore's Memorial and Counter-Memorial, no reference is made expressly to the status of Pedra Branca/Pulau Batu Puteh as terra nullius, the Court observes that in its Reply Singapore expressly indicated that "[i]t is obvious that the status of Pedra Branca in 1847 was that of terra nullius".

In light of the foregoing, the Court notes that the issue is reduced to whether Malaysia can establish its original title dating back to the period before Singapore's activities of 1847 to 1851, and conversely whether Singapore can establish its claim that it took "lawful possession of Pedra Branca/Pulau Batu Puteh" at some stage from the middle of the nineteenth century when the construction of the lighthouse by agents of the British Crown started.

The question of the burden of proof (paras. 43-45)

On this question, the Court reaffirms that it is a general principle of law, confirmed by its jurisprudence, that a party which advances a point of fact in support of its claim must establish that fact.

Legal status of Pedra Branca/Pulau Batu Puteh before the 1840s (paras. 46-117)

– Original title to Pedra Branca/Pulau Batu Puteh (paras. 46-80)

The Court starts by observing that it is not disputed that the Sultanate of Johor, since it came into existence in 1512, established itself as a sovereign State with a certain territorial domain under its sovereignty in part of south-east Asia. Having examined the arguments of the Parties, the Court notes that, from at least the seventeenth century until early in the nineteenth, it was acknowledged that the territorial and maritime domain of the Kingdom of Johor comprised a considerable portion of the Malaya Peninsula, straddled the Straits of Singapore and included islands and islets in the area of the Straits — where Pedra Branca/Pulau Batu Puteh is located.

The Court then moves to ascertain whether the original title to Pedra Branca/Pulau Batu Puteh claimed by Malaysia is founded in law.

Of significance is the fact that Pedra Branca/Pulau Batu Puteh had always been known as a navigational hazard in the Straits of Singapore. Therefore the island evidently was not terra incognita. The fact that there is no evidence throughout the entire history of the old Sultanate of Johor that any competing claim had ever been advanced over the islands in the area of the Straits of Singapore is another significant factor.

The Court recalls the pronouncement made by the Permanent Court of International Justice (PCIJ) in the case concerning the Legal Status of Eastern Greenland, on the significance of the absence of rival claims. The PCIJ then noted that, while "[i]n most of the cases involving claims to territorial sovereignty … there have been two competing claims to the sovereignty", in the case before it "up to 1931 there was no claim by any Power other than Denmark to the sovereignty over Greenland". The PCIJ therefore concluded that, considering the "inaccessible character of the uncolonized parts of the country, the King of Denmark and Norway displayed … in 1721 to 1814 his authority to an extent sufficient to give his country a valid claim to sovereignty, and that his rights over Greenland were not limited to the colonized area".

The Court observes that this conclusion also applies to the present case involving a tiny uninhabited and uninhabitable island, to which no claim of sovereignty had been made by any other Power throughout the years from the early sixteenth century until the middle of the nineteenth century. In that context the Court also notes that State authority should not necessarily be displayed "in fact at every moment on every point of a territory", as shown in the Island of Palmas Case (Netherlands/United States of America).

The Court concludes from the foregoing that the territorial domain of the Sultanate of Johor covered in principle all the islands and islets within the Straits of Singapore, including the island of Pedra Branca/ Pulau Batu Puteh. It finds that this possession of the islands by the Sultanate was never challenged by any other Power in the region and can in all the circumstances be seen as satisfying the condition of "continuous and peaceful display of territorial sovereignty". The Court thus concludes that the Sultanate of Johor had original title to Pedra Branca/ Pulau Batu Puteh.

Examining the ties of loyalty that existed between the Sultanate of Johor and the Orang Laut ("the people of the sea"), who were engaged in fishing and piratical activities in the Straits of Singapore, the Court finds that the descriptions, in contemporary official reports by British officials, of the nature and the level of relationship between the Sultan of Johor and the Orang Laut confirm the ancient original title of the Sultanate of Johor to those islands, including Pedra Branca/Pulau Batu Puteh.

The Court then turns to the question whether this title was affected by the developments in the period 1824 to 1840.

–   The legal significance of the 1824 Anglo-Dutch Treaty (paras. 81-101)

First the Court notes that documentary evidence conclusively shows that the Sultanate of Johor continued to exist as the same sovereign entity throughout the period 1512 to 1824, in spite of changes in the precise geographical scope of its territorial domain and vicissitudes of fortune in the Sultanate through the ages, and that these changes and vicissitudes did not affect the legal situation in relation to the area of the Singapore Straits, which always remained within the territorial domain of the Sultanate of Johor.

Second, the Court observes that it is common ground between the Parties that the 1824 Anglo-Dutch Treaty divided the region into two parts — one belonging to the Dutch sphere of influence (the Riau-Lingga Sultanate under Abdul Rahman) and the other falling under the British sphere of influence (the Sultanate of Johor under Hussein). However, Singapore appears to claim that the Treaty left the entire Straits aside, and that Pedra Branca/Pulau Batu Puteh had remained terra nullius or had become terra nullius as a result of the division of the "old Sultanate of Johor", thus leaving room for the "lawful possession" of Pedra Branca/ Pulau Batu Puteh by the British during the period 1847–1851.

After careful analysis of the text of the 1824 Anglo-Dutch Treaty, the Court concludes that the Treaty was the legal reflection of a political settlement reached between the two colonial Powers to divide the territorial domain of the old Sultanate of Johor into two sultanates to be placed under their respective spheres of influence. Thus in this scheme there was no possibility for any legal vacuum left for freedom of action to take lawful possession of an island in between these two spheres of influence.

The general reference in Article 12 of the Treaty to "the other Islands south of the Straights of Singapore" would suggest that all the islands and islets within the Straits fell within the British sphere of influence. This naturally covered the island of Pedra Branca/Pulau Batu Puteh, which thus remained part of what continued to be called the "Sultanate of Johor" after the division of the old Sultanate.

‒   The relevance of the 1824 Crawfurd Treaty (paras. 102-107)

The Court considers the relevance to the dispute of the "Crawfurd Treaty", by which the Sultan and Temenggong of Johor ceded the island of Singapore to the East India Company. The Court states that the Treaty cannot be relied on as establishing "British recognition of prior and continuing sovereignty of the Sultanate of Johor over all other islands in and around the Strait of Singapore", including Pedra Branca/ Pulau Batu Puteh, as Malaysia claimed. The Court however notes that this finding does not signify a contrario that the islands in the Straits of Singapore falling outside the scope of Article II of this Treaty were terrae nullius and could be subject to appropriation through "lawful occupation" either. This latter point can only be judged in the context of what legal effect the division of the old Sultanate of Johor had upon the islands in the area of the Straits of Singapore, in particular in light of the 1824 Anglo-Dutch Treaty and in light of the legal relevance, vel non, of the so-called letter "of donation" of 1825 sent from Sultan Abdul Rahman of Riau-Lingga to his brother Sultan Hussein of Johor.

‒   The legal significance of the letter "of donation" of 1825 (paras.
    108-116)

The Court examines whether the letter "of donation" from Sultan Abdul Rahman to his brother Hussein had the legal effect of transferring the title to the territory included in that letter "of donation". The Court notes that the so-called letter "of donation" from Sultan Abdul Rahman to his brother Hussein merely confirmed the division agreed upon by the 1824 Anglo-Dutch Treaty and therefore was without legal effect.

‒   Conclusion (para. 117)

The Court concludes that Malaysia has established to its satisfaction that as of the time when the British started their preparations for the construction of the lighthouse on Pedra Branca/Pulau Batu Puteh in 1844, this island was under the sovereignty of the Sultan of Johor.

Legal status of Pedra Branca/Pulau Batu Puteh after the 1840s (paras. 118-272)

The Court observes that in order to determine whether Malaysia has retained sovereignty over Pedra Branca/Pulau Batu Puteh following 1844 or whether sovereignty has since passed to Singapore, it needs to assess the relevant facts — consisting mainly of the conduct of the Parties during that period — by reference to the governing principles and rules of international law.

−   Applicable law (paras. 118-125)

It notes that any passing of sovereignty might be by way of agreement between the two States in question. Such an agreement might take the form of a treaty, as with the 1824 Crawfurd Treaty and the 1927 Agreement referred to earlier. The agreement might instead be tacit and arise from the conduct of the Parties. In this matter international law does not impose any particular form but places its emphasis on the parties' intentions. Sovereignty over territory might under certain circumstances pass as a result of the failure of the State which has sovereignty to respond to conduct à titre de souverain of the other State or to concrete manifestations of the display of territorial sovereignty by the other State. Such manifestations of the display of sovereignty may call for a response if they are not to be opposable to the State in question. The absence of reaction may well amount to acquiescence. That is to say, silence may also speak, but only if the conduct of the other State calls for a response. Critical for the Court's assessment of the conduct of the Parties is the central importance in international law and relations of State sovereignty over territory and of the stability and certainty of that sovereignty. Because of that, any passing of sovereignty over territory on the basis of the conduct of the Parties must be manifested clearly and without any doubt by that conduct and the relevant facts.

−   The process for the selection of the site for Horsburgh lighthouse (paras. 126-148)

In 1836 merchants and mariners expressed the wish to build one or more lighthouses in memory of James Horsburgh, a hydrographer to the East

Indies Company. In November 1836 "Pedra Branca" was identified as a preferred location. In a letter sent to the Governor of Singapore on 1 March 1842 "Pedra Branca" was the only locality specifically mentioned. The Court notes that, in this first formal communication, the private commercial interests recognized that the British Government would have to carry the proposal into effect and provide the further funds.

In the ensuing correspondence between the subscribers and the British authorities several alternative locations were envisaged. By October 1844, the island of Peak Rock was identified as the most eligible site. In late November W.J. Butterworth, who had become Governor of the Straits Settlements in 1843, received replies to letters which he had written to the Sultan and Temenggong of Johor. Notwithstanding the Parties' extensive research, the Governor's letters have not been found, but the Parties did provide to the Court copies of the translations of the replies, both dated 25 November 1844, in which the Sultan and the Temenggong consented to the construction of a lighthouse in the Straits of Singapore, without mentioning the exact location.

Examining whether Johor ceded sovereignty over the particular piece of territory which the United Kingdom would select for the construction and operation of the lighthouse for the stated purpose or granted permission only to that construction and operation, the Court finds that the correspondence is not conclusive.

Given the lack of any written agreement relating to the modalities of the maintenance of the lighthouse and the island on which it was to be constructed, the Court considers that it is not in a position to resolve the issue about the content of any possible agreement reached in November 1844.

– The construction and commissioning of Horsburgh lighthouse, 1850–1851 (paras. 149-163)

The Court notes that the planning for the construction and the construction itself were in the hands of the Government Surveyor of Singapore, John Thomson, who was appointed as Architect of the project by Governor Butterworth. In December 1849 the Government Surveyor began organizing the construction. On 24 May 1850 the foundation stone was laid. The Court takes note of the fact that no Johor authorities were present at the ceremony. There is no indication that they were even invited by the Governor to attend. That might suggest that the British and Singapore authorities did not consider it necessary to apprise Johor of their activities on Pedra Branca/Pulau Batu Puteh. The Temenggong of Johor visited the rock only once, nine days after the laying of the foundation stone, accompanied by 30 of his followers.

After describing the modalities of the construction and commissioning of the lighthouse, the Court notes that it cannot draw any conclusions with regard to sovereignty. Rather it sees those events as bearing on the issue of the evolving views of the authorities in Johor and in Singapore about sovereignty over Pedra Branca/Pulau Batu Puteh.

–   The conduct of the Parties, 1852-1952 (paras. 164-191)

The Court first considers the <u>Straits lights system and related British and Singapore legislation</u>. It notes that as a matter of law, a lighthouse may be built on the territory of one State and administered by another State — with the consent of the first State. A central element in Malaysia's argument is that because Horsburgh lighthouse was built on an island over which Johor was sovereign all the actions of the British authorities and, following them, the Singaporean authorities, are simply actions pursued in the normal course of the operation of the lighthouse. Singapore, by contrast, says that some of the actions are not matters simply of the operation of the lighthouse but are, in whole or part, acts <u>à titre de souverain</u>. Singapore refers to legislation enacted by itself and its predecessors in title, which regulated the defraying of costs of establishing and operating the lighthouse, vesting control of it under various governmental bodies, and regulating the activities of persons residing, visiting and working on Pedra Branca/Pulau Batu Puteh. In the Court's view however the provisions invoked by Singapore do not as such demonstrate British sovereignty over the areas to which they apply, because they applied equally to lighthouses which are undoubtedly on Johor territory as well as to that on Pedra Branca/Pulau Batu Puteh and, moreover, say nothing expressly about sovereignty.

Turning to the various <u>constitutional developments</u> invoked by Malaysia, including the 1927 Straits Settlement and Johor Territorial Waters Agreement, the Court considers that they do not help resolve the question of sovereignty over Pedra Branca/Pulau Batu Puteh. It observes that the purpose of the Agreement was to "retrocede" to Johor certain areas that had been ceded by Johor to the East India Company in 1824 and were all within 10 miles of the main island of Singapore. They could not have included Pedra Branca/Pulau Batu Puteh, as the island was not within the scope of the Agreement.

With respect to Malaysia's contention that the Temenggong continued to control fishing in the neighbourhood of Pedra Branca/Pulau Batu Puteh after the construction of the lighthouse, as shown by an exchange of correspondence between Johor and the British authorities in Singapore in 1861, the Court observes that the letters relate to events occurring within 10 miles of the island of Singapore. Therefore nothing can be made of the fact that the Singapore authorities did not in that context refer to jurisdiction over the waters of Pedra Branca/Pulau Batu Puteh.

–   The 1953 correspondence (paras. 192-230)

The Court notes that on 12 June 1953 the Colonial Secretary of Singapore wrote to the British Adviser to the Sultan of Johor, that he was "directed to ask for information about the rock some 40 miles from Singapore known as Pedra Branca" in the context of "the determination of the boundaries of the Colony's territorial waters". Acknowledging that in the case of Pulau Pisang, an island "which is also outside the Treaty limits of the colony" it was "clear that there was no abrogation of the sovereignty of Johore", the Secretary asked to be informed of "any document showing a lease or grant of the rock or whether it ha[d] been ceded by the Government of the State of Johore or in any other way disposed of". Later in that month the Secretary to the British Adviser to the Sultan of Johor advised the Colonial Secretary that he had passed the letter to the State Secretary of Johor, who would "doubtless wish to consult with the Commissioner for Lands and Mines and Chief Surveyor and any existing archives before forwarding the views of the State Government to the Chief Secretary". In a letter dated 21 September 1953, the Acting State Secretary of Johor replied that "the Johore Government [did] not claim ownership of Pedra Branca".

The Court considers that this correspondence and its interpretation are of central importance for determining the developing understanding of the two Parties about sovereignty over Pedra Branca/Pulau Batu Puteh.

The Court notes that the Singapore letter of 12 June 1953 seeks information about "the rock" as a whole and not simply about the lighthouse in light of the determination of the Colony's territorial waters, a matter which is dependent on sovereignty over the island. The Court notes that the letter had the effect of putting the Johor authorities on notice that in 1953 the Singapore authorities understood that their predecessors thought that Pedra Branca/Pulau Batu Puteh had been ceded "gratuitously" by the Sultan and the Temenggong to the East India Company. The Court reads the letter as showing that the Singapore authorities were not clear about events occurring over a century earlier and that they were not sure that their records were complete.

Turning to the reply from the Acting State Secretary of Johor, the Court dismisses the Malaysian contention that, under the provisions of the Johor Agreement between the British Crown and the Sultan of Johor and the Federation of Malaya Agreement between the British Crown and nine Malay states (including Johor), the Acting State Secretary "was definitely not authorized" and did not have "the legal capacity to write the 1953 letter, or to renounce, disclaim, or confirm title of any part of the territories of Johore".

The Court considers that the Johor Agreement is not relevant since the correspondence was initiated by a representative of Her Britannic Majesty's Government which at that time was not to be seen as a foreign State; further, it was the British Adviser to the Sultan of Johor who passed the initial letter on to the Secretary of State of the Sultanate. The Court is also of the view that the Federation of Malaya Agreement does not assist the Malaysian argument because the action of responding to a request for information is not an "exercise" of "executive authority". Moreover, the failure of Malaysia to invoke this argument, both throughout the whole period of bilateral negotiations with Singapore and in the proceedings until late in the oral phase, lends support to the presumption of regularity invoked by Singapore.

Examining the 1953 letter's content, the Court expresses the view that the Johor reply is clear in its meaning: Johor does not claim ownership over Pedra Branca/Pulau Batu Puteh. That response relates to the island as a whole and not simply to the lighthouse. When the Johor letter is read in the context of the request by Singapore for elements of information bearing on the status of Pedra Branca/Pulau Batu Puteh, as discussed above, it becomes evident that the letter addresses the issue of sovereignty over the island. The Court accordingly concludes that Johor's reply shows that as of 1953 Johor understood that it did not have sovereignty over Pedra Branca/Pulau Batu Puteh. In light of Johor's reply, the authorities in Singapore had no reason to doubt that the United Kingdom had sovereignty over the island.

The steps taken by the Singapore authorities in reaction to the final response were not known to the Johor authorities and have limited significance for the Court's assessment of any evolving understanding shared by the Parties. The case file shows that, on receipt of the Johor reply, the Colonial Secretary of Singapore sent an internal memorandum to the Attorney-General saying that he thought that "[o]n the strength of [the reply], we can claim Pedra Branca ..." The Attorney-General stated that he agreed. The Singapore authorities, so far as the case file shows, took no further action. They had already received related communications from London, to which the Court now turns.

–   The conduct of the Parties after 1953 (paras. 231-272)

The Court first takes into consideration Singapore's contention that it and its predecessors have exercised sovereign authority over Pedra Branca/Pulau Batu Puteh by investigating shipwrecks within the island's territorial waters. Concluding that this conduct gives significant support to the Singapore case, the Court also recalls that it was only in June 2003, after the Special Agreement submitting the dispute to the Court had come into force that Malaysia protested against this category of Singapore conduct.

After examining the argument of Singapore's exercise of exclusive control over visits to Pedra Branca/Pulau Batu Puteh and the use of the island by officials from Singapore as well as from other States, including Malaysia, the Court states that many of the visits by Singaporean personnel related to the maintenance and operation of the lighthouse and are not significant in the case. However it finds that the conduct of Singapore with respect to permissions granted or not granted to Malaysian officials in the context of a survey of the waters surrounding the island in 1978 is to be seen as conduct à titre de souverain and does give significant support to Singapore's claim to sovereignty over Pedra Branca/Pulau Batu Puteh.

Both Parties contend that their naval patrols and exercises around Pedra Branca/Pulau Batu Puteh since the formation of their respective navies constitute displays of their sovereign rights over the island. The Court does not see this activity as significant on one side or the other. It observes that naval vessels operating from Singapore harbour would as a matter of geographical necessity often have to pass near Pedra Branca/Pulau Batu Puteh.

As for Singapore's claim that the flying of the British and Singapore ensigns from Horsburgh lighthouse from the time of its commissioning to this day is also a clear display of sovereignty, the Court states that the flying of an ensign is not in the usual case a manifestation of sovereignty. It considers that some weight may nevertheless be given to the fact that Malaysia did not protest against the ensign flying at Horsburgh lighthouse.

The Court then looks into the installation of a relay station by the Singapore Navy, in May 1977, for a military rebroadcast station on Pedra Branca/Pulau Batu Puteh. Singapore contends that the installation was carried out openly. Malaysia asserts that the installation was undertaken secretly and that it became aware of it only on receipt of Singapore's Memorial. The Court is not able to assess the strength of the assertions made on the two sides about Malaysia's knowledge of the installation. The conduct is inconsistent with Singapore recognizing any limit on its freedom of action.

As for the plans to reclaim areas around Pedra Branca/Pulau Batu Puteh, which had been considered on various occasions in the 1970s by the Port of Singapore Authority, the Court observes that while the reclamation was not proceeded with and some of the documents were not public, the tender advertisement was public and attracted replies. Further the proposed action, as advertised, did go beyond the maintenance and operation of the lighthouse. It is conduct which supports Singapore's case.

In 1968 the Government of Malaysia and the Continental Oil Company of Malaysia concluded an agreement authorizing petroleum exploration in the whole of the area of the continental shelf off the east coast of West Malaysia. Given the territorial limits and qualifications in the concession and the lack of publicity of the co-ordinates, the Court does not consider that weight can be given to the concession.

By legislation of 1969 Malaysia extended its territorial waters from 3 to 12 nautical miles. Malaysia contends that the legislation "extended Malaysian territorial waters to and beyond Pulau Batu Puteh". The Court notes however that the said legislation does not identify the areas to which it is to apply except in the most general sense: it says only that it applies "throughout Malaysia".

Malaysia invokes several territorial agreements to support its claim to sovereignty over Pedra Branca/Pulau Batu Puteh: the Indonesia Malaysia Continental Shelf Agreement of 1969, the Territorial Sea Agreement of 1970 and the Indonesia Singapore Territorial Sea Agreement of 1973. The Court does not consider that those agreements can be given any weight in respect of sovereignty over Pedra Branca/Pulau Batu Puteh, since they did not cover this issue. The Court similarly does not see as significant for the purposes of the proceedings the co-operation in the Straits of Malacca and Singapore adopted in 1971 by Indonesia, Malaysia and Singapore, which was invoked by Singapore.

The Court also dismisses as non-authoritative and essentially descriptive certain official publications of the Government of Singapore describing its territory, which in the view of Malaysia are notable for their absence of any reference to Pedra Branca/Pulau Batu Puteh among the approximately 60 islands that are included in those descriptions.

Finally, the Court turns to nearly a hundred official maps submitted by the Parties. Malaysia emphasizes that of all the maps before the Court only one published by the Singapore Government included Pedra Branca/Pulau Batu Puteh as within its territory and that map was not published until 1995. The Court recalls that Singapore did not, until 1995, publish any map including Pedra Branca/Pulau Batu Puteh within its territory. But that failure to act is in the view of the Court of much less weight than the weight to be accorded to the maps published by Malaya and Malaysia between 1962 and 1975. The Court concludes that those maps tend to confirm that Malaysia considered that Pedra Branca/Pulau Batu Puteh fell under the sovereignty of Singapore.

Conclusion (paras. 273-277)

The Court is of the opinion that the relevant facts, including the conduct of the Parties, reflect a convergent evolution of the positions of the Parties regarding title to Pedra Branca/Pulau Batu Puteh. The Court concludes, especially by reference to the conduct of Singapore and its predecessors à titre de souverain, taken together with the conduct of Malaysia and its predecessors including their failure to respond to the conduct of Singapore and its predecessors, that by 1980 sovereignty over Pedra Branca/Pulau Batu Puteh had passed to Singapore.

For the foregoing reasons, the Court concludes that sovereignty over Pedra Branca/Pulau Batu Puteh belongs to Singapore.

Sovereignty over Middle Rocks and South Ledge (paras. 278-299)

Arguments of the Parties (paras. 278-287)

The Court notes that Singapore's position is that sovereignty in respect of Middle Rocks and South Ledge goes together with sovereignty over Pedra Branca/Pulau Batu Puteh. Thus, according to Singapore, whoever owns Pedra Branca/Pulau Batu Puteh owns Middle Rocks and South Ledge, which, it claims, are dependencies of the island of

Pedra Branca/Pulau Batu Puteh and form with the latter a single group of maritime features. Malaysia on the other hand argues that these three features do not constitute one identifiable group of islands in historical or geomorphological terms, and adds that they have always been considered as features falling within Johor/Malaysian jurisdiction.

Legal status of Middle Rocks (paras. 288-290)

The Court first observes that the issue of the legal status of Middle Rocks is to be assessed in the context of its reasoning on the principal issue in the case. It recalls that it has reached the conclusion that sovereignty over Pedra Branca/Pulau Batu Puteh rests with Singapore under the particular circumstances surrounding the case. However these circumstances clearly do not apply to other maritime features in the vicinity of Pedra Branca/Pulau Batu Puteh, i.e., Middle Rocks and South Ledge. None of the conduct of the Parties reviewed in the previous part of the Judgment has any application to the case of Middle Rocks.

The Court therefore finds that original title to Middle Rocks should remain with Malaysia as the successor to the Sultan of Johor.

Legal status of South Ledge (paras. 291-299)

With regard to South Ledge, the Court however notes that there are special problems to be considered, inasmuch as South Ledge presents a special geographical feature as a low-tide elevation.

The Court recalls Article 13 of the United Nations Convention on the Law of the Sea and considers its previous jurisprudence, the arguments of the Parties, as well as the evidence presented before it.

The Court notes that South Ledge falls within the apparently overlapping territorial waters generated by the mainland of Malaysia, by Pedra Branca/Pulau Batu Puteh and by Middle Rocks. It recalls that in the Special Agreement and in the final submissions it has been specifically asked by the Parties to decide the matter of sovereignty separately for each of the three maritime features. At the same time the Court observes that it has not been mandated by the Parties to draw the line of delimitation with respect to the territorial waters of Malaysia and Singapore in the area in question.

In these circumstances, the Court concludes that sovereignty over South Ledge, as a low-tide elevation, belongs to the State in the territorial waters of which it is located.

Operative clause (para. 300)

"For these reasons,

THE COURT,

(1)   By twelve votes to four,

Finds that sovereignty over Pedra Branca/Pulau Batu Puteh belongs to the Republic of Singapore;

IN FAVOUR: Vice-President, Acting President, Al-Khasawneh; Judges Ranjeva, Shi, Koroma, Buergenthal, Owada, Tomka, Keith, Sepúlveda-Amor, Bennouna, Skotnikov; Judge ad hoc Sreenivasa Rao;

AGAINST: Judges Parra-Aranguren, Simma, Abraham; Judge ad hoc Dugard;

(2)   By fifteen votes to one,

Finds that sovereignty over Middle Rocks belongs to Malaysia;

IN FAVOUR: Vice-President, Acting President, Al-Khasawneh; Judges Ranjeva, Shi, Koroma, Parra-Aranguren, Buergenthal, Owada, Simma, Tomka, Abraham, Keith, Sepúlveda-Amor, Bennouna, Skotnikov; Judge ad hoc Dugard;

AGAINST: Judge ad hoc Sreenivasa Rao;

(3)   By fifteen votes to one,

Finds that sovereignty over South Ledge belongs to the State in the territorial waters of which it is located.

IN FAVOUR: Vice-President, Acting President, Al-Khasawneh; Judges Ranjeva, Shi, Koroma, Buergenthal, Owada, Simma, Tomka, Abraham, Keith, Sepúlveda-Amor, Bennouna, Skotnikov; Judges ad hoc Dugard, Sreenivasa Rao;

AGAINST: Judge Parra-Aranguren.

Judge Ranjeva appends a declaration to the Judgment of the Court; Judge Parra-Aranguren appends a separate opinion to the Judgment of the Court; Judges Simma and Abraham append a joint dissenting opinion to the Judgment of the Court; Judge Bennouna appends a declaration to the Judgment of the Court; <u>Judge</u> ad hoc Dugard appends a separate opinion to the Judgment of the Court; <u>Judge</u> ad hoc Sreenivasa Rao appends a separate opinion to the Judgment of the Court.

* * * * *

Declaration of Judge Ranjeva

Judge Ranjeva considers that no substantive objection can be raised to the present Judgment, in so far as Malaysia's immemorial historical title to Pedra Branca/Pulau Batu Puteh is established, even though Singapore's sovereignty over this feature at the date of the Court's decision cannot reasonably be contested. That however is not the case for the Court's reasoning in respect of the transfer of Johor's sovereignty to Singapore. Judge Ranjeva thus points out that the purpose of his declaration is to suggest an alternative basis on which the Court could have relied.

In the present Judgment, the Court infers acquiescence on the part of Johor to the transfer of its title of sovereignty over Pedra Branca/ Pulau Batu Puteh. In Judge Ranjeva's view, there are only two events from which a transfer of sovereignty can result: either an equivalent act occurs (the possibility referred to in paragraph #120 of the Judgment), or a superior legal title intervenes. In the absence of the latter situation, Judge Ranjeva wonders how Johor's title could have been extinguished without Johor's consent. For lack of evidence, the Judgment relies on presumptive consent to reach the conclusion that sovereignty was transferred; this is open to criticism as being out of keeping with the facts.

Judge Ranjeva believes that the Judgment came to this conclusion through a failure to take account of the historical criticism approach in interpreting the facts in their contemporary political and legal context. While relations between sovereign colonial Powers fell within the ambit of international law, it is difficult to argue that dealings between the United Kingdom and the Sultanate of Johor were based on relations between sovereign, equal subjects of international law. Thus, the sovereignty acknowledged to indigenous authorities was inoperative vis-à-vis colonial Powers, the authorities' sole obligation being to submit to the will of the Powers. Under these circumstances, the Sultan of Johor could not broach the slightest opposition to a decision by the British. Judge Ranjeva thus considers that the present case cannot be seen as involving an international transfer of title by the operation of acquiescence, when, under the rules and practice of the colonial Powers, what was involved was the exercise of a colonial territorial title. Johor's silence through the colonial period cannot therefore be held against it. The situation changed however with the Parties' accession to independence: Malaysia may no longer rely on its silence in response to conduct pointing towards Singapore's sovereignty over Pedra Branca/Pulau Batu Puteh. In conclusion, Singapore has sovereignty over the island.

Separate opinion of Judge Parra-Aranguren

I

1.   Judge Parra-Aranguren considers that the findings made by the Court in its Judgment demonstrate that juridical reasons can always be found to support any conclusion.

II

2.   Judge Parra-Aranguren voted against paragraph 300 (1) of the Judgment because it is based mainly on the interpretation of the 1953 correspondence made in section 5.4.5, which he cannot accept.

3.   On 12 June 1953 Singapore asked Johor for information in an attempt to clarify the status of Pedra Branca/Pulau Batu Puteh owing to the island's relevance to the determination of Singapore's territorial waters; it asked in particular whether there was any document showing a lease or grant, or whether the island had been ceded by Johor or in any other way disposed of. The Acting State Secretary of Johor replied on 21 September 1953, informing Singapore that "the Johore Government does not claim ownership of Pedra Branca" (paras. 192 and 196 of the Judgment).

4.   Singapore maintained that, "'by declaring that Johor did not claim Pedra Branca, the [Johor State Secretary's] letter had the effect of confirming Singapore's title to Pedra Branca and of confirming that Johor had no title, historic or otherwise, to the island'". Moreover, Singapore stressed that its argument was not "that Johor abandoned or relinquished title to Pedra Branca in 1953" and that the effect of Johor's 1953 letter was "to pronounce explicitly that Johor did not have a claim to ownership of Pedra Branca".

5.   In this respect Judge Parra-Aranguren recalls that in earlier sections of the Judgment the Court concluded that prior to 1953

Pedra Branca/Pulau Batu Puteh belonged to Malaysia and for this reason, in his opinion, the Johor's 1953 letter could not have had the effect of confirming either that Singapore held title to Pedra Branca/Pulau Batu Puteh or that Johor had no title to Pedra Branca/Pulau Batu Puteh, as maintained by Singapore.

6. Singapore did not maintain that the 1953 letter should be understood as Johor's renunciation, abandonment or relinquishment of its title to Pedra Branca/Pulau Batu Puteh and, accordingly, Judge Parra-Aranguren believes that this argument should not have been analysed and relied upon to conclude that Singapore holds title to Pedra Branca/Pulau Batu Puteh.

7. As paragraph 196 of the Judgment states: "No further correspondence followed and the Singapore authorities took no public action."

8. In the opinion of Judge Parra-Aranguren, it is surprising that "[n]o further correspondence followed", because Johor had not furnished the information requested by Singapore and the basic practice in international relations whenever a question remains unanswered is to repeat the request in writing and to insist that the information be provided. Singapore chose not to proceed in this way and did not explain to the Court why it abstained from acting.

9. Furthermore, the 1953 letter from Johor answered a completely different question from the one asked by Singapore, merely stating that "the Johor Government does not claim ownership of Pedra Branca". Paragraph 222 of the Judgment acknowledges that "ownership" is in principle distinct from "sovereignty", but that "[i]n international litigation 'ownership' over territory has sometimes been used as equivalent to 'sovereignty'". It is a fact that Johor used the term "ownership", not "sovereignty". Therefore, in Judge Parra-Aranguren's view, if Singapore understood the 1953 letter to mean in reality that Johor did "not claim sovereignty over Pedra Branca", it should at the very least, have requested the explanation from Malaysia necessary to "clarify the status of Pedra Branca", which was Singapore's main objective in sending the letter of 12 June 1953.

10.   The lack of "public action" by Singapore's authorities is more difficult to understand than the "lack of further correspondence".

11.   In the opinion of Judge Parra-Aranguren, if Singapore did in fact consider that its sovereignty over Pedra Branca/Pulau Batu Puteh had been acknowledged, notwithstanding the ambiguous terms of Johor's 1953 letter, elementary principles of good faith required Singapore to assert a formal claim of sovereignty over Pedra Branca/Pulau Batu Puteh, especially in the light of the facts mentioned in paragraphs 196 and 224 of the Judgment. However, Singapore failed to do so and, as a result of its inaction, the status of Pedra Branca/Pulau Batu Puteh, far from being "clarified", remained obscure.

12.   Additionally, it may be observed that, while information about Pedra Branca/Pulau Batu Puteh was sought because it was "relevant to the determination of the boundaries of the Colony's territorial waters", no action was taken, as acknowledged in paragraph 225 of the Judgment.

III

13.   Judge Parra-Aranguren also voted against paragraph 300 (1) of the Judgment because he does not agree with the examination of "[t]he conduct of the Parties after 1953" made in section 5.4.6.

14.   In this section the Court states that the United Kingdom and Singapore acted as operator of Horsburgh Lighthouse, but "that was not the case in all respects"; also, "[w]ithout being exhaustive", the Court recalls actions to have been performed by Singapore à titre de souverain. However "the bulk of them" took place after 1953, as stated in paragraph 274 of the Judgment, and the Court has already determined in its Judgment dated 10 October 2002, that a period of some 20 years is "far too short" (Land and Maritime Boundary between Cameroon and Nigeria (Cameroon v. Nigeria: Equatorial Guinea intervening), Judgment, I.C.J. Reports 2002, p. 352, para. 65). In the present case the Court finds in paragraph 34 of the Judgment that 14 February 1980 is the critical date for the purposes of the dispute as to sovereignty over Pedra Branca/

Pulau Batu Puteh. Therefore, even assuming that the actions mentioned in section 5.4.6 of the Judgment were performed by Singapore à titre de souverain, the period concerned is "far too short" and for this reason, in Judge Parra-Aranguren's opinion, they are not sufficient to undermine Johor's historical title to Pedra Branca/Pulau Batu Puteh. Singapore's effectivités do not correspond to the law, and, as the Court has reiterated more than once, "[w]here the act does not correspond to the law, where the territory which is the subject of the dispute is effectively administered by a State other than the one possessing the legal title, preference should be given to the holder of the title" (Frontier Dispute (Burkina Faso/Republic of Mali), Judgment, I.C.J. Reports 1986, p. 587, para. 63).

15.   Paragraph 275 of the Judgment states that "the Johor authorities and their successors took no action at all on Pedra Branca/Pulau Batu Puteh from June 1850 for the whole of the following century or more". Similar statements are also found in a number of other paragraphs of the Judgment and were made repeatedly by Singapore in the present proceedings. However, in the opinion of Judge Parra-Aranguren, the Johor authorities and their successors were under no international obligation to undertake any action at all, because Johor had historical title to Pedra Branca/Pulau Batu Puteh, as recognized in the Judgment. On the contrary, clarification of the status of the island was a matter of prime importance to Great Britain, because Great Britain had made a substantial investment in the construction and maintenance of Horsburgh lighthouse. However, Great Britain remained silent over the years and the status of Pedra Branca/Pulau Batu Puteh was still unclear in 1953, as evidenced in Mr. J.D. Higham's letter.

IV

16.   Paragraph 297 of the Judgment states that the Court "will proceed on the basis of whether South Ledge lies within the territorial waters generated by Pedra Branca/Pulau Batu Puteh, which belongs to Singapore, or within those generated by Middle Rocks, which belongs to Malaysia"; and "that South Ledge falls within the apparently overlapping territorial waters generated by the mainland of Malaysia, Pedra Branca/Pulau Batu Puteh and

Middle Rocks". The Court adds in paragraph 298 that "in the Special Agreement and in the final submissions it has been specifically asked to decide the matter of sovereignty separately for each of the three maritime features", but at the same time observes that it "has not been mandated by the Parties to draw the line of delimitation with respect to the territorial waters of Malaysia and Singapore in the area in question". Consequently in paragraph 300 (3) of the Judgment the Court "[f]inds that sovereignty over South Ledge belongs to the State in the territorial waters of which it is located."

17.   As explained above, Judge Parra-Aranguren considers that Pedra Branca/Pulau Batu Puteh belongs to Malaysia and he agrees that Middle Rocks is under the sovereignty of Malaysia, as found in paragraph 300 (2) of the Judgment. Therefore, in his opinion South Ledge is located within the territorial waters of Malaysia and for this reason it belongs to Malaysia. Consequently, he voted against paragraph 300 (3) of the Judgment.

V

18.   On 23 November 2007 the Court informed Malaysia and Singapore that it was retiring for deliberation. Public hearings on the merits in the case brought by Djibouti against France commenced on 21 January 2008 and the Court retired eight days later for deliberation, which is ongoing. Public hearings on the Preliminary Objections in the case concerning Application of the Convention on the Prevention and Punishment of the Crime of Genocide (Croatia v. Serbia and Montenegro), to be held from 26 to 30 May 2008, require careful examination beforehand of the written arguments and of some requests made by the Parties.

19.   Judge Parra-Aranguren therefore wishes to emphasize that constraints arising from the time-limits fixed by the Court for the preparation of this separate opinion have prevented him from setting out a thorough explanation of his disagreement with sub-paragraphs (1) and (3) of paragraph 300 and that he has for this reason only described some of the main reasons why he has voted against them.

Joint dissenting opinion of Judges Simma and Abraham

Judges Simma and Abraham express their disagreement with the first point of the operative clause of the Judgment which attributes the island of Pedra Branca/Pulau Batu Puteh to Singapore.

They endorse the conclusion reached by the Court at the end of the first part of its reasoning, whereby in 1844, on the eve of the construction of the Horsburgh lighthouse, the island was under the sovereignty of the Sultanate of Johor.

However, they dissociate themselves from the Judgment when it indicates that, between 1844 and 1980, sovereignty passed to Singapore, as a result of conduct of the Parties reflecting a convergent evolution of their positions as regards the status of the island.

Firstly, Judges Simma and Abraham note that the Court refrains from indicating clearly on which legal basis it relies to justify such a change in the holder of sovereignty, in the absence of any express agreement between the States concerned. In the abstract presentation that it gives of the applicable law, the Judgment refers to the possibility of a "tacit agreement" or of "acquiescence" by the original sovereign, but it makes no choice between these in the concrete conclusion that it draws from an examination of the conduct of the Parties, nor does it indicate if and how it might be possible for them to be combined. Further, the Judgment makes no mention of the notion of "acquisitive prescription", which appears capable of accounting for the process whereby a State acquires sovereignty over a territory that did not originally belong to it and without the express consent of the original sovereign.

Judges Simma and Abraham nonetheless take the view that, in substance, the Judgment draws on the criteria which they hold to be legally correct in order to assess the conduct of the Parties, even if it does not refer clearly enough to the relevant legal categories, which is not the most important point.

However, Judges Simma and Abraham disagree with the way in which the Judgment applies those criteria to the present case, and, consequently, with the conclusions that it draws from them.

Indeed, the facts do not demonstrate a sufficiently clear, consistent and public exercise of State sovereignty over the island by Singapore and its predecessor Great Britain, so that no acquiescence of any kind to the transfer of sovereignty can be deduced from the lack of reaction by Malaysia and its predecessor Johor.

According to Judges Simma and Abraham, there are thus at least two conditions lacking for the application of acquisitive prescription —

or of tacit agreement, or acquiescence, since those legal categories are not hermetically separated from one another — namely, on the one hand, the effective exercise of the attributes of sovereignty by the State relying on them (Singapore in this case) combined with the intention to act as sovereign and, on the other hand, the visibility of this exercise of sovereignty, making it possible to establish the acceptance, through its lack of reaction, of the original sovereign (Malaysia in this case).

The acts taken into consideration by the Court as manifestations of sovereignty by Singapore are minor and sporadic, and their meaning was far from clear from the perspective of Johor and Malaysia. The Court should therefore not have concluded that sovereignty over the island had passed to Singapore. It should have attributed it to Malaysia, as the undisputed successor of the Sultanate of Johor.

Declaration of Judge Bennouna

Judge Bennouna, who voted in favour of the operative clause in the Judgment, is nevertheless not convinced by all of the reasoning adopted by the Court in justifying it. After reviewing the doubts entertained by the Court whenever it has looked to colonial law in its past decisions, Judge Bennouna expresses his view that the Court should have relied in the present case essentially on the practice of the two States after Singapore gained independence in 1965 further to its withdrawal from the Federation of Malaysia, which had been established in 1963. In Judge Bennouna's opinion, the Court would thus have avoided deciding on the basis of colonial practices resulting by and large from the rivalry between two European Powers seeking to secure their hegemony in the region.

Dissenting opinion of Judge <u>ad hoc</u> Dugard

Judge Dugard dissents on the question of sovereignty over Pedra Branca/Pulau Batu Puteh, but concurs with the Court in respect of its finding that Malaysia has territorial title to Middle Rocks and that South Ledge is to be disposed of in accordance with the law governing maritime territorial delimitation.

Judge Dugard agrees with the Court that Malaysia had original title to Pedra Branca/Pulau Batu Puteh and finds that neither the conduct of Malaysia nor that of Singapore between 1850 and 1980 has disturbed this title. In particular, he finds that the 1953 correspondence between

Johor and Singapore did not result in, or contribute to, the passing of sovereignty from Johor to Singapore. Judge Dugard argues that the conduct of both Parties between 1953 and 1980 is equivocal and cannot be interpreted to indicate that Malaysia had abandoned title to Pedra Branca/Pulau Batu Puteh or acquiesced in Singapore's assertion of title over the island.

Judge Dugard is critical of the legal reasons advanced by the Court to support its finding that sovereignty passed from Johor/Malaysia to Singapore. He finds that notions of tacit agreement, arising from the conduct of the Parties, developing understanding between the Parties and acquiescence are not supported by the facts and do not provide an acceptable legal foundation upon which to base the passing of sovereignty over Pedra Branca/Pulau Batu Puteh from Johor/Malaysia to Singapore.

Separate opinion of Judge ad hoc Sreenivasa Rao

Judge ad hoc Sreenivasa Rao, partially dissenting, explained his reasons for finding that sovereignty over Middle Rocks should also have been attributed to Singapore. In his view, Malaysia failed to meet the burden of proof incumbent upon it to establish that Johor had original title over Pedra Branca/Pulau Batu Puteh and the other two maritime features, Middle Rocks and South Ledge. In his view, the general historical description of the Malay Kingdom cannot be taken as certain and convincing evidence that Johor ever considered these maritime features as its possessions. Any claim of immemorial possession, to succeed, must first establish effective uninterrupted and uncontested possession. In the absence of evidence in favour of such possession, Johor at best could be held to have had an inchoate title based on discovery which it did not, however, perfect. For this, it required to display peaceful and continuous State authority commensurate with the nature of the territory involved. Activities of the Orang Laut, in so far as they are accepted as subjects of Johor, are private and do not account for display of Johor's State authority. The Orang Laut's piratical activities are even more inadmissible as evidence for the purpose of establishing the original title of Johor.

He further noted that Singapore, in contrast, exercised various State functions with respect to Pedra Branca/Pulau Batu Puteh and exercised control over waters around it for over 130 years, after it took over possession of the same in 1847. Accordingly, even though at the time

Britain took possession of Pedra Branca/Pulau Batu Puteh it was <u>not</u> <u>terra nullius</u>, by virtue of the exhibition of superior <u>effectivités</u> for over a period of 130 years Britain/Singapore could be held to have manifested sovereignty over it and the waters around it. Accordingly, Singapore acquired title which it maintained without interruption and contest. Johor's reply to Singapore in 1953 stating that it did not claim any ownership over the rock confirms this. By virtue of such sovereignty over Pedra Branca/Pulau Batu Puteh and the waters around it, Singapore also has sovereignty over Middle Rocks and South Ledge as these maritime features fall within the limits of the territorial waters of Singapore.

INDEX